CREATIVE WRITING

By
CAROLYN KANE, Ph.D.

COPYRIGHT © 1994 Mark Twain Media, Inc.

Printing No. CD-1855

Mark Twain Media, Inc., Publishers
Distributed by Carson-Dellosa Publishing Company, Inc.

The purchase of this book entitles the buyer to reproduce the student pages for classroom use only. Other permissions may be obtained by writing Mark Twain Media, Inc., Publishers.

All rights reserved. Printed in the United States of America.

Creative Writing

TABLE OF CONTENTS

INTRODUCTION 1

PART ONE: Getting Started 2
    1. Looking for Ideas 2
    2. You Are the Expert 4
    3. Show, Don't Tell! 6
    4. Choosing Verbs That Work 8

PART TWO: Thinking About People 10
    5. The Characters in Your Story 10
    6. Choosing the Right Names for Your Characters 12
    7. Everyone's Favorite Things 14

PART THREE: Planning a Story 16
    8. Plot and Conflict 16
    9. Making Good Use of Conflict 18
    10. Dialogue: Listening to the Characters Talk 20
    11. Dialogue: A Few Reminders 22
    12. Setting: The Scene of the Action 24
    13. Writing Effective Description 26
    14. Research Can Be Fun 28

PART FOUR: Thinking About Words 30
    15. Build Your Vocabulary 30
    16. The Tools Writers Use 34
    17. Be Brief! 36
    18. How to Use Figures of Speech 38
    19. Diction: Words That Say What You Mean 40

PART FIVE: Imagination 42
    20. Let Your Mind Soar! 42
    21. Don't Be Yourself! 44
    22. A New World 46
    23. Let's Make a Deal—Now! 48
    24. Tall Tales 50

PART SIX: Writing Your Story 52
    25. Writing and Revising 52
    26. Planning the Outline 56
    27. Drawing the Characters 59

PART SEVEN: What Writers Do 61
    28. Writing a Book Review 61
    29. Writing a Short Newspaper Article 63
    30. The Dreaded Research Paper! 65
    31. Writing About Your Opinions 67
    32. Doing an Interview 69
    33. Keeping a Diary 71
    34. Writing Letters 73
    35. Getting Published 75
    36. Postscript—The Writers' Club 77

Creative Writing

INTRODUCTION

This activity book is designed to take the student through the step-by-step process of creating and writing a short story. The opening section is an introduction to a few of the basic maxims of creative writing: Write about what you know; show, don't tell; use strong verbs. The second and third sections present some of the main elements of fiction: characterization, plot, dialogue, setting, and description. Each chapter contains exercises to help a novice writer gain practice and build confidence.

Good writing involves both careful craftsmanship and imaginative freedom. Therefore, the fourth and fifth sections are intended to complement each other. Part Four deals mainly with craftsmanship and especially with the choice of appropriate words, while Part Five contains readings and exercises designed to stimulate the student's imagination. In Part Six, the student outlines a plot for a story, writes a short sketch of the main character, and then writes the story.

A few of the chapters are meant to prepare the student for future assignments; such a chapter is "The Dreaded Research Paper!" in Part Seven. Other chapters are not so much instructions to students as brief glimpses into the life of a professional writer. These chapters include "The Tools Writers Use" in Part Four and some of the material in Part Seven, which is entitled "What Writers Do."

In writing this book, I received some useful suggestions from Heidi Dierckx and Vanessa Bennett and also from Robert and Carol Mathieson, who contributed most of the "inventions" in the chapter entitled "Let's Make a Deal—Now!" In particular, I would like to express my appreciation to Sandy Asher—author, teacher, and workshop leader—who has been a source of inspiration over the years.

This book is dedicated to my parents, John and Katherine Kane, who provided me with a firm foundation for a good career and a good life.

—THE AUTHOR

© Mark Twain Media, Inc., Publishers

Creative Writing

PART ONE: GETTING STARTED

1. Looking for Ideas

Have you ever wanted to be a writer? Do you enjoy reading, hearing, and telling stories? Have you ever dreamed of seeing your words and your name in print? If so, there are a number of things you can do, starting today, that may someday turn your dream into reality—and that "someday" may come sooner than you think.

The *short story* is a good place to begin. Let us consider the most basic ingredient of the story: an idea. People will often ask a writer, "Where do you get your ideas?" These people seem to imagine that every professional writer knows of a secret place where "ideas" grow wild like mushrooms, free for the picking. Late at night when nobody is looking, the writer sneaks out into the darkness, tiptoes to his secret idea garden, plucks a batch of mushroom-ideas, stashes them in a brown paper bag, and carries them home to his study. Actually, the search for ideas is a good deal simpler than cultivating and harvesting a crop of edible mushrooms. Ideas are everywhere. For most successful writers, the best source of ideas is personal experience.

Often a story idea begins with a person. Try to think of the most interesting people you have ever known. What about your cousin Nicholas, who owns five hundred horror-film videos, has watched each of them fifty times, and is building a replica of a mad scientist's laboratory in the basement of his parents' home? Would he make a good character in a story? What if one of his make-believe experiments actually succeeded? Or consider your Aunt Stella, the lead singer of the worst jazz band in the history of St. Louis. How would she react if, by some miracle, she made a recording that became a hit? Then there's your friend Heather, who is curious about everything and remembers the name of everyone she has ever met. She might make a good heroine in a detective story.

Places can also be good sources of ideas. What places do you know? Is there a mysterious empty building in your neighborhood? Do you enjoy spending the summer at your uncle's farm? Do you like to visit the planetarium or the zoo or the museum? Have you ever considered the possibility that your school building might be haunted by the ghost of a dead principal?

You might build a story around your own favorite activities and interests. If you sometimes get up early in the morning for a game of basketball with your friends, then perhaps you should try writing a story about basketball. If you like computers, maybe you would prefer to write science fiction. If you find teddy bears irresistible, you might write an exciting tale about how a rare teddy bear is stolen from a museum. Whatever your hobby or interest may be, chances are that you can find a way to write a story about it. Once you start thinking about the people, places, and events of your life, you will see that stories are all around you.

Creative Writing PART ONE: Getting Started; Looking for Ideas

Date _____ Name _____

ASSIGNMENT: Looking for Ideas

Take stock of your personal experience by answering the following questions. When you are finished, you should have a page filled with ideas for stories.

1. Who are the three most interesting people I have ever known?
_____
_____

2. What person do I most admire?
_____

3. What are my three favorite places in the entire word? (A "place" might be an entire state or city, or it might simply be a room, a building, or a playground.)
_____
_____

4. What places do I like the least?
_____
_____

5. What were the happiest or most exciting moments of my life?
_____

6. What was the most frightening moment of my life?
_____

7. What was the most embarrassing moment of my life?
_____

8. When did I learn something new and interesting?
_____

9. If Aladdin's genie offered to grant me three wishes, what would they be?
_____
_____

Creative Writing

PART ONE: GETTING STARTED

2. You Are The Expert

When teachers and professional writers are asked for advice, they often say, "Write about what you know." To this a typical person might reply, "But I don't know about anything. I'm just a bookbinder, not a spy or a rocket scientist, and I live in a boring little town where nothing ever happens." But everyone has some kind of knowledge, and so do you, although you may not realize it.

If you started in scouting as a Tiger Cub, you are an expert on the Boy Scouts. If you have taken piano lessons for several years, you probably know the meanings of words like *andante* and *glissando,* and you know how to give a piano recital. If you live on a farm, you know more about animals than most people do—and almost everyone loves to read about animals. On the other hand, maybe you are a person who knows and understands the life of crowded, big-city streets. If you are good at taking care of your little sister while your mother is at work, if you play in a marching band, or if you live in a place where flooding is common, you have a story that is worth telling.

Don't be too quick to assume that your experiences would be boring to read about. You may live in a dull, dusty little town with only a thousand citizens, but remember that to a person who has spent his entire life in the city, your home town might seem strange and even scary. (Suppose the city dweller found a copperhead curled up on the porch or a skunk in the back yard! And would he know what to do if a tornado should strike?) Garrison Keillor, a modern writer, made himself famous by telling and writing stories about life in a fictitious small town called Lake Wobegon, Minnesota (population 946). Likewise, you might think of bookbinding as a dull life, but Lilian Jackson Braun wrote a murder mystery, *The Cat Who Sniffed Glue,* in which one of the characters is a mild-mannered bookbinder who repairs rare volumes, keeps a gun on the shelf over his sink, and may not be as harmless as he looks. A good writer can make almost any subject seem interesting.

One of the first things a writer must do is take stock of his knowledge. Start thinking about what you have studied, practiced, and learned from experience. Do you have a favorite subject in school? Have you ever cared for an unusual pet? Can you play a musical instrument? Do you like to build or collect things? After you have answered questions such as these, you will probably realize that you have plenty of information to write about, and you won't hesitate to follow the writer's standard advice:

"Write about what you know."

Creative Writing   PART ONE: Getting Started; You Are the Expert

Date _____ Name _____

ASSIGNMENT: Finding Out What You Know

To discover where your knowledge lies, list some of the ways in which you have gained information and understanding:

1. Jobs you have held _____

2. Jobs your relatives have held _____

3. Favorite subjects in school _____

4. Lessons in music, dancing, or art _____

5. Things you like to read about _____

6. Organizations you have joined _____

7. Sports you have played _____

8. Things you see every day _____

9. Pets that you or your family have had _____

Creative Writing

PART ONE: GETTING STARTED

3. Show, Don't Tell!

Suppose you want to write a story about a boy named Chadwick, who is so clumsy that he can hardly walk into a room without tripping over the rug, or pick up a glass of lemonade without spilling it. You might begin your story by simply telling your readers about Chadwick's problem, like this:

> *Chadwick was clumsy. He got good grades in school, but he was always doing things that made him feel stupid. Most of the time he felt so embarrassed that he was afraid to meet people and make friends.*

This is a short, clear beginning, but isn't it a bland and colorless description of Chadwick? And won't the reader be confused about what "things" Chadwick does to cause himself so much distress? Your story will be more exciting or amusing or sad if you follow the most important rule of creative writing: **show, don't tell.** Instead of telling your readers that Chadwick was bright but clumsy, let them see Chadwick in action:

> *Chadwick stumbled into Harry's Hamburger Heaven and ordered a double cheeseburger and a milkshake. He decided to join Frank and Nancy at their booth; maybe they would be impressed when he showed them the medal he had won at the science fair. But when he picked up his tray and started toward the booth, he tripped over the doormat and fell to his knees. His cheeseburger landed in a pot of ferns, and his milkshake splattered all over the football coach. Laughter rang through the dining room. Chadwick blinked back tears as he scrambled to his feet and ran out of the restaurant, leaving his gold medal on the floor where it had fallen.*

After your readers have seen this paragraph, they won't have to be geniuses to figure out that Chadwick was smart, clumsy, and lonely.

Here is another example. *Telling:* "Anne had a miserable case of the flu." *Showing:* "Anne coughed until her ribs ached. She shivered as she wiped her nose for the hundredth time and reached for another cough drop." Which version makes you feel greater sympathy for Anne?

When you write a story, try to picture your characters in action. Some writers like to take walks along busy streets and sit in crowded restaurants where they can watch how people walk, talk, dress, and behave. Later they may jot down notes on what they have seen, so that they can use this material in stories or articles. People-watching could be the most inexpensive hobby you will ever have, and one that will help you develop your writing skills. If you become a keen observer of people, you will quickly learn to *show* instead of *tell*.

© Mark Twain Media, Inc., Publishers

Creative Writing — PART ONE: Getting Started; Show, Don't Tell!

Date _____ Name _____

ASSIGNMENT: Show, Don't Tell!

Rewrite one of the following paragraphs and make it more vivid by showing instead of telling:

1. Alice's room was a mess. All kinds of stuff was piled everywhere. Even Alice couldn't find anything in all that clutter.

_____
_____
_____
_____

2. Mr. Mudge is a dull teacher. His students never learn anything because they are so bored. Even the other teachers are bored by Mr. Mudge.

_____
_____
_____
_____

3. Ralph's Bar-B-Q is the worst restaurant in town. The food is so bad that I hate to eat there, and so do my friends. I don't think Ralph's cooking is healthy, either.

_____
_____
_____
_____

4. Allen studies too much. He doesn't have time to make friends because he is too busy studying. He doesn't get any exercise, either. All of his friends and relatives are worried about him.

_____
_____
_____
_____
_____
_____

Creative Writing

PART ONE: GETTING STARTED

4. Choosing Verbs That Work

Verbs are a writer's best friends. Strong verbs can fill your sentences and stories with life, because the action of your tale is in the verbs. On the other hand, weak verbs can make even a good story seem slow and tedious. One of the first lessons a writer must learn is how to select verbs that are filled with action.

Fortunately, the English dictionary is crammed with lively verbs. Think, for example, of all the different ways that a speaker of English can travel by foot: he can walk, run, race, charge, saunter, wander, meander, traipse, trudge, limp, stagger, stumble, or swagger. (Can you add any words to this list?) How many ways do we laugh? We can chuckle, chortle, cackle, snicker, giggle, titter, guffaw, howl, hoot, roar, or even split our sides. Think how we might sit in our chairs: we can lounge, loll, sprawl, slump, perch, hunch, or recline. We might even fall asleep, and then we could doze, nap, snooze, slumber, snore, or just pass out.

If you want your writing to be entertaining and interesting, you should avoid the *passive voice* whenever you can. For example, never write "The football was kicked by Andy" when you can write "Andy kicked the football." Notice that the second version is shorter and simpler; it sounds more like action, more like kicking. Verbs such as *am, is, are, was,* and *were* are valuable words, but they are weak. Avoid them when you are describing vigorous action. Never write "There was a tornado approaching Springfield" or "A tornado was seen approaching Springfield." Write instead, "The tornado swirled toward Springfield" or "The tornado smashed into Springfield, shattering houses to splinters and tossing cars as if they were dead leaves." Whenever possible, avoid beginning your sentences with the words *there are, there is,* and *there were.* Instead of saying "There were a great many people at the football game," say instead, "Hundreds of people crowded into the football stadium."

Words like *come, go, went,* and *gone* are also useful, but they add little to a description. Instead of writing "The horse went across the field," it would be better to say that the horse ambled, trotted, cantered, galloped, raced, tore, or pounded across the field. Also, whenever possible, beware of using a tame verb with the word *not.* For example, instead of saying that "Albert did not like math," you might say that he hated, detested, or loathed math, or that he shuddered at the thought of working math problems.

Try making a list of the strongest verbs you can think of. When you read or watch television, look and listen for good verbs and write them down. You will soon discover that the English language has more than enough colorful verbs to keep you and your characters busy for years.

Creative Writing — PART ONE: Getting Started; Choosing Verbs That Work

Date _____ Name _____

ASSIGNMENT: Using Strong Verbs

Revise the following sentences, changing weak verbs into strong ones:

1. There was a sound of gunfire in the street.

2. Eight fire engines and two ambulances could be seen going toward Scrooge Tower.

3. Dan took the football and went toward the goal line. The opponents came after him and tried to stop him from scoring.

4. There was rain all morning, and in the afternoon hail was heard at the window.

5. At her ballet lessons, Amy did not dance very gracefully. At the end of a lesson, she was not usually smiling with satisfaction.

6. The front door made a noise as Jennifer went into the haunted house and looked around. There were cobwebs and dust everywhere. Cracked windows and tattered curtains were seen by Jennifer when she went into the dining room. A mysterious noise could be heard from the tower. Was it possible that a ghost would come down the staircase?

Using as many strong verbs as possible, describe one of the following: a basketball game, a parade, a Halloween party, a dog show, an automobile accident, a house fire.

© Mark Twain Media, Inc., Publishers

Creative Writing

PART TWO: THINKING ABOUT PEOPLE

5. The Characters in Your Story

Remember Nicholas, the story character who has seen every horror film ever made, owns the videos of most of them, and is building a life-sized replica of Dr. Frankenstein's laboratory in his parents' basement? Let us say that he is going to be the hero of a story that you will entitle "My Cousin the Mad Scientist." Because Nicholas is the hero, he must have many good and endearing qualities, so that your readers will like him enough to enjoy spending time with him.

What are his best qualities? Obviously, Nicholas is intelligent and has the gift of imagination. Imaginative people usually make enjoyable friends; they can also create works of art and solve problems. Nicholas has dedication, enough that he can devote hours, weeks, and years to a beloved hobby instead of getting bored and losing interest quickly, as many people would. He is talented at building things and determined to succeed at whatever he does. And he is brave—maybe too brave for his own good if he plans to create a monster in the very house where he lives. All in all, Nicholas is quite an admirable young man.

But if you want your readers to believe that a person like Nicholas could really exist, he will have to have flaws in his character, just as real people do. A perfect person, if one existed, would be almost impossible to talk to, let alone make friends with. So before you start writing "My Cousin the Mad Scientist," stop and think: What are your hero's weaknesses?

Does Nicholas always hand in his homework on time? Probably not, because he is so busy puttering and rattling around in the basement that he completely forgets about his assignments. Sometimes he even forgets that he is sitting in his algebra class; he gazes dreamily into space and loses himself in visions of werewolves and zombies. Even though he is one of the smartest students in school, his teachers often lose patience with him—and so do his parents, because he is too busy cataloging his horror videos to rake the lawn. Even *you* (his cousin) get annoyed with Nicholas when he forgets his promise to help you study for an algebra test.

The best characters are usually mixtures of good and bad qualities. Even the most wicked villain is likely to have at least one admirable quality; otherwise, how can the hero take him seriously? Consider the villain of your story, the mysterious Professor Zilch, who is trying to steal an invention created by Nicholas. Professor Zilch is dishonest, greedy, devious, selfish, arrogant, and possibly even cruel. Does he have any good qualities? Well, he's intelligent and daring, and he probably has enough charm that he can almost succeed in winning Nicholas's trust. And however evil he may be, at least he isn't lazy. Stealing inventions is hard work!

© Mark Twain Media, Inc., Publishers

Creative Writing   PART TWO: Thinking About People; The Characters in Your Story

Date _____   Name _____

ASSIGNMENT: Creating a Believable Character

You are writing a story about Vanessa Archer, who dreams of becoming a famous singer. Vanessa's mother says that music lessons are too expensive and that most musicians are poor. She wants Vanessa to learn about computers so that she can get a good job and help support her younger brothers and sisters. Without telling her mother, Vanessa joins the school choir and tries out for a solo part. Then she goes to the church on the corner of her block, finds the choir director, and persuades him to give her some free lessons.

1. If you were going to write this story, what would Vanessa's good qualities be?

a. _____

b. _____

c. _____

e. _____

f. _____

2. What do you think might be the weaknesses in Vanessa's character?

a. _____

b. _____

c. _____

3. What would be the most admirable thing about Mrs. Archer, Vanessa's mother?

_____

4. What is the most serious flaw in Mrs. Archer's character?

_____

5. How do you think the story will turn out?

_____

_____

_____

_____

_____

Creative Writing

PART TWO: THINKING ABOUT PEOPLE

6. Choosing the Right Names for Your Characters

The choice of a character's name is an important decision, so think about it carefully. Once you have devised a name for your leading character, you will probably be stuck with your choice; it will be almost impossible for you to think of him or her with a different name, just as it would be difficult for you to start calling your friend Jack by the name "Trevor." An important thing to remember is that your character's name should fit his personality and his way of life. Fictional characters often seem to have minds of their own, and if you give a character the wrong name, he may become stubborn and refuse to carry out his role in your story.

For example, if your heroine lives on a farm and is especially good at working with pigs, it would probably be a bad idea to name her "Jasmine" or "Mercedes." Can you really picture someone named "Mercedes" getting up at five in the morning to slop the hogs? Maybe this character should have a down-to-earth name like "Kate" or "Tess" or "Sue." If your hero is a defensive tackle on a professional football team, your readers will find it strange if his name should turn out to be "Ethelbert Quimby." If your leading character is a glamourous film star with a hundred jeweled dresses in her closet, the names "Griselda" and "Dousabel" would be bad choices for her. Or suppose she is a woman of mystery, free as the wind and secretive as the night? You had better not call her "Mary Smith." And will anyone believe in a vampire named "Pete" or "Hank"?

Fortunately, there are ways to find interesting and suitable names for your characters. For example, you might consult a good name-the-baby book, where you will find the familiar names like *Jane* and *Robert* along with some names that are not so familiar, such as *Allegra, Fiona, Germaine,* and *Marelda* for girls, and *Brandon, Cosmo, Kendrick,* and *Ellery* for boys. If you are looking for a solid-sounding name for a sympathetic character, you might consult the Bible for such fine old names as *Adam, Michael, David, Daniel, Mark, Hannah, Rebecca, Sarah, Ruth,* and *Esther.* History can also give you clues. For a dignified heroine, you might choose "Catherine" or "Elizabeth" after the famous empress of Russia or queen of England. Or you might call her "Regina," which is the Latin word for "queen." For family names, check the telephone directory. Here, side by side with the Joneses and the Smiths and the Wilsons, you will also find the Awerkamps, the Buckalews, the Diffendaffers, the Quesenberrys, the Scharnhorsts, and the Zwicks.

A word of warning: *Never* name a character after a real person—not even a character who has all of the best qualities of Superman, Albert Einstein, and Elvis Presley—because the person whose name you use may feel embarrassed and uncomfortable because of your choice. And be very, very careful about how you name your villains. For example, don't name your villainess "Betty," because for all you know, half of your readers might also be called "Betty." It will be easier for your readers to get into the spirit of your story if you pick an off-beat name such as "Aurelia" or "Nerine" or "Gweneth." You will run little risk of offending anyone with a villainess named "Aurelia Glitch."

© Mark Twain Media, Inc., Publishers

Creative Writing PART TWO: Thinking About People; Choosing the Right Names for Your Characters

Date _____ Name _____

ASSIGNMENT: Thinking About Names

Study the following names for characters in a story and try to decide what sort of personality would fit each name.

1. Alice Whiffle _____
_____

2. Robert Franklin _____
_____

3. Biff Snorkle _____
_____

4. Jennifer Browning _____
_____

5. Kermit Hinkle _____
_____

6. Jordan Michaelson _____
_____

7. Fern Summers _____
_____

8. Arthur Noble _____
_____

9. Zippo Measley _____
_____

10. Lewis Clark _____
_____

11. Antoinette Glitz _____
_____

© Mark Twain Media, Inc., Publishers

Creative Writing

PART TWO: THINKING ABOUT PEOPLE

7. Everyone's Favorite Things

You make a decision every time you buy something, keep it, throw it away, clean it, let it gather dust, hide it, or put it on display. Through your decisions, you reveal your character. If you have a shelf full of books about cats, a wall covered with cat posters, and a cat-shaped alarm clock that meows instead of rings, it will be no secret to your friends that you love cats.

Like real people, fictional characters reveal themselves through their clothes and other possessions. If you want to create memorable characters, try to get a clear picture of what they look like, what clothes they wear, what sorts of books and television programs they enjoy, and what things are scattered around their homes. Can you picture Nicholas, the teenaged mad scientist? Chances are, he is so busy thinking about science that he keeps forgetting to shop for new clothes or get a haircut. His sweater is starting to come unraveled in a few places, and occasionally he has to push a lock of hair away from his face. He's a bit thin, because sometimes he even forgets to eat. In his pocket he carries a pen and a pad of paper (for writing down brilliant ideas) and a library card. Now imagine his bedroom, which is cluttered with movie posters, books about science and the history of film, science fiction magazines, videotapes, batteries, coils of wire, and boxes of tools. If you give a brief description of Nicholas's room, your readers will quickly get an idea about what sort of person he is.

People also reveal character through the things they don't own and don't buy. Suppose Nicholas meets a man who claims that he was once a great chef in a famous restaurant. On and on he talks about how he used to cook dinner for movie stars and how he once cooked a gourmet meal for the President of the United States. Later, Nicholas and his family visit the home of this "chef." Nicholas discovers that his host has not a single cookbook on his shelves and no box of recipes on his kitchen cabinet and that all of his pots and pans look as if he bought them at a junk shop. If you were Nicholas, wouldn't you suspect that the "great chef" was lying about his past? So would most readers.

But appearances can be deceiving. It's usually a bad idea to judge people too quickly, either in life or in fiction. Maybe the chef is a liar; maybe not. Perhaps he misses his exciting life at the restaurant so much that he can't bear to be reminded of it when he is at home, and so he has given away all of his cookbooks and sold his gleaming pans and skillets. A serious student of human nature must keep his mind open to all of the possibilities.

So think carefully about what your characters wear, own, and do without. Sometimes it's the small details that bring a character to life.

© Mark Twain Media, Inc., Publishers

Creative Writing   PART TWO: Thinking About People; Everyone's Favorite Things

Date _____ Name _____

ASSIGNMENT: People and Things

1. Christmas is coming, and Felix would like to have the following gifts: a new guitar, a pair of good running shoes, a *Three Stooges* video, a blanket and water bowl for his dog, a book of free passes to a movie theatre, and two books entitled *How to Improve Your Low Grades Without Cheating* and *So You Want to Be a Clown!* What sort of person is Felix? Do you think he will make a good clown?

_____
_____
_____
_____

2. You find the following items in a man's desk: a magnifying glass, a membership card for a gun collector's club, several odd-looking rocks, a new passport, a gold-plated letter opener, a pipe and some smoking tobacco, a slip of paper with a Bulgarian telephone number written on it, a note that says "Call the Museum of Science and Industry before two o'clock," and a laundry bill that should have been paid two weeks ago. On his desk is a framed picture of a Siamese cat. What sort of man is this? What do you suppose he does for a living? Do you think he is married?

_____
_____
_____
_____

3. The following items can be found in and around the Robinson's family room and kitchen: a cabinet full of oat bran cereal and vegetable juice, a refrigerator full of "Healthy Life" brand frozen dinners, a baseball bat, several copies of a magazine called *Horse and Rider,* about fifty notes and reminders on the bulletin board, more notes on the refrigerator, some crayon drawings hanging on the wall, comfortable chairs and couches, a full bookshelf, an AM-FM radio, and a compact disk player. What sort of people are the Robinsons? What familiar item is missing from their family room? Would you enjoy being a member of this family?

_____
_____
_____
_____

Creative Writing

PART THREE: PLANNING A STORY

8. Plot and Conflict

A *plot* is the foundation on which a writer builds his story. A strong plot creates excitement, captures a reader's interest, and keeps him turning the pages eagerly. But plot is more than simple action. A good plot also gives the characters an opportunity to reveal their personalities—their strengths and weaknesses, their skills and incompetence, their good or wicked natures. After all, how can a reader get to know the characters if they never have anything significant to do?

When we say that a story has a plot, we usually mean that a conflict takes place. At the center of the conflict is the main character, who is called the *protagonist.* It is important to remember the difference between the words "protagonist" and "hero" or "heroine." If we say that a character named Fred is the "hero" of a story, we are suggesting that Fred is wholeheartedly on the side of goodness and truth and that he probably possesses such attractive qualities as intelligence, strength, ingenuity, and good looks. If Fred is the "protagonist," on the other hand, he could be any sort of person under the sun—smart or stupid, handsome or ugly, energetic or lazy, good or evil. The only requirement is that he be the central figure in a significant conflict.

A good storyteller must be aware of the variety of conflicts available to him. Probably the most common type of story is the one in which the protagonist comes into conflict with another person. A good example is the story of the great detective Sherlock Holmes and his battle of wits with the evil Professor Moriarty. Another popular type of story deals with a man or woman in conflict with nature or natural forces. For over 200 years, readers around the world have enjoyed the tale of Robinson Crusoe and his lonely struggle to survive on a desert island. Other protagonists may come into conflict, not with man or nature, but with themselves. In William Shakespeare's play *Macbeth,* the protagonist undergoes an agonizing struggle with his own conscience as he plots to murder the king and usurp the throne.

In science fiction, the protagonist is sometimes threatened by a machine or by some other aspect of technology: a robot that goes awry and runs amok, or a super-intelligent computer that mysteriously develops a mind of its own (or, for a more light-hearted fantasy, a telephone system that rings only wrong numbers). Or the protagonist might find himself confronting an impossible creature, like a werewolf or a three-headed alien from outer space. Some protagonists might even have to struggle against an entire society. For example, the protagonist might be a heroine who is the defendant in a witchcraft trial, or she might be a runaway slave trying to escape to freedom on the Underground Railroad, or a young girl trying to save her brother from getting involved with a street gang. Or the conflict with society might be real but less dramatic. In the Disney film *Beauty and the Beast,* the heroine is a small-town girl who yearns to escape from her quiet life into a wide world of adventure and romance. Her neighbors have no desire to harm her; but, because she is different from everyone else, they find it impossible to understand and appreciate her.

The person or force against which the protagonist struggles is called the *antagonist.* The antagonist is often a villain, but not always. If the protagonist were a bloodthirsty vampire, the hunter who tracks and kills the creature could be a good or heroic character. Or the antagonist might be a decent but misinformed person—somebody who wants to do the right thing but doesn't know how. Sometimes the most interesting stories are those in which two admirable characters come into conflict with each other.

Creative Writing   PART THREE: Planning a Story; Plot and Conflict

Date _____ Name _____

ASSIGNMENT: Thinking About Conflict

1. Write down the names of three favorite books or short stories. What was the most important conflict in each of them?
_____
_____
_____

2. Everyone experiences conflict from time to time. What kinds of conflict do you encounter in your daily life? (Arguments with friends and family members? Struggles to get good grades, make the basketball team, or just get yourself out of bed in the morning?)
_____
_____
_____

3. Have you ever had to struggle against a force of nature? Explain.
_____
_____

4. Have you ever had a major conflict within yourself—a struggle to overcome fear or make a difficult decision? Explain.
_____
_____

5. Have you ever had a conflict with a group of people? Explain.
_____
_____

6. Have you ever had to struggle against a machine? Explain.
_____
_____

7. Which of these conflicts would make the best stories? Why?
_____
_____
_____
_____

Creative Writing

PART THREE: PLANNING A STORY

9. Making Good Use of Conflict

It is sometimes a good idea to have two or more conflicts in the same story. Suppose you were writing a story about a young amateur sleuth named Heather. She was born and raised in Chicago, but she takes a summer job on her uncle's farm, where a famous archaeologist and her students have found well-preserved artifacts of a vanished Indian society. A mysterious man in green-tinted spectacles keeps hanging around the area. Sometimes he claims to be a "developer"; at other times he identifies himself as a "consultant." Heather does not trust him, and she begins to suspect that her uncle's farm conceals a secret more valuable than arrowheads, pipe stems, and grinding stones.

Consider the possible conflicts. If Heather is the protagonist, the man in the green glasses will probably be the chief antagonist, and the main conflict will be a battle of their two minds. But you can bring in other conflicts as well. Heather will have to struggle against nature as she searches for artifacts (and clues to the mystery) in the blazing summer heat. She will have a struggle within herself as she tries to adjust to farm life; sometimes it will be all she can do to keep herself from jumping on the next train back to Chicago, where she feels at home. She might even come into conflict with some elements of society, because the world is still full of people who think that archaeology and sleuthing are not suitable activities for girls!

When you write your story, you should introduce your protagonist as soon as possible—the first sentence is not too soon. And if possible, your first paragraph should contain some hint of the conflicts to come:

> Heather Franklin shaded her eyes against the July sun. Had it been her imagination, or had she seen a man in green-tinted glasses slip into Geisendorfer's Country Market through the back door? Heather shook her head in disbelief. She doubted that anything mysterious could possibly happen at this sleepy crossroads, so far from her home town of Chicago.

The main conflict should begin quickly and grow more intense as the story progresses. Near the end of the tale, the struggle should build to its moment of greatest intensity, called the *climax*, in which the protagonist either triumphs or fails. It is important to remember that if the protagonist is to win, she should succeed because of her own efforts. It would be a bad idea to end your story by letting Heather get rescued by a sheriff who just happens to wander past the farm at the right moment. In the first place, no one will believe that Heather could be so lucky, and in the second place, the rescue won't be much of a victory for Heather. If she is to be rescued, she must at least be smart enough to send a Morse code message with a flashlight or find some way of getting to a telephone to call for help.

Creative Writing   PART THREE: Planning a Story; Making Good Use of Conflict

Don't make the common mistake of building carefully to an exciting climax and then rushing past the "big" scene in two or three sentences: *Quickly Heather aimed her trusty flashlight at Sheriff Brady's house and flashed the SOS signal. Five minutes later she sighed with relief to see the sheriff come hurrying across the dark field, accompanied by his faithful German Shepherd.* Your reader will feel cheated by such an abrupt and brief resolution of the danger. He wants to share Heather's heart-pounding fear as she searches in the dark for her flashlight, her worry about whether the batteries will still be good, her tension as she hears the crunch of footsteps against dry grass—is it the friendly sheriff or someone more sinister?—and her giddy relief when she recognizes the familiar bark of the sheriff's dog.

Date _____ Name _____

ASSIGNMENT: Conflicts of Different Sorts

Invent names for characters who match the following descriptions. What sort of conflicts would these characters probably encounter?

1. a veterinarian who lives in the country _____
_____

2. a girl who wants to be a scientist _____
_____

3. an injured football player _____
_____

4. a brilliant detective who is afraid of the dark _____
_____

5. the head majorette in a marching band _____
_____

6. a teacher at a junior high school _____
_____

7. a lazy man who likes to lie on the porch and read magazines all day _____
_____

Creative Writing

PART THREE: PLANNING A STORY

10. Dialogue: Listening to the Characters Talk

The word *dialogue* (also spelled *dialog*) refers to conversation among your characters. The first thing to remember about dialogue is that you ought to make use of it. Your story will be dull and unconvincing if the characters never talk to each other. Even if your hero has no one to talk to because he is crossing the Atlantic Ocean alone in a ten-foot sailboat, he can make a few remarks to himself from time to time, talk to a friendly dolphin, or chat with his fellow mariners over a short-wave radio.

Your characters should talk, but not too much. A character who rambles on for an entire page is definitely overdoing it. And a story that consists almost entirely of dialogue will be boring indeed, unless the writer happens to be a genius. To get an idea of how much dialogue is enough, look carefully at the works of writers whom you particularly enjoy. Notice the methods they use to keep their fiction from becoming too "talky." Sometimes a skillful writer will break up long blocks of dialogue with brief bits of description:

> *Heather glanced away from Mr. Geisendorfer, trying not to hear his angry words. On the other side of the dry creek, the fields lay parched and yellow from the summer heat. The Queen Anne's lace drooped by the side of the road, and even the scarecrow looked exhausted.*

Or you might try a brief glimpse into a character's thoughts and memories:

> *As Heather listened to Mr. Geisendorfer's angry words, she thought longingly of her old job at Bixby's Cafe, a pleasant place filled with bustle, laughter, and music. Mr. Bixby had been kindness itself. His harshest criticism was "Maybe you should try just a little harder next time."*

A character's spoken words should fit his or her personality. If a character named Angela is a nun, don't let her swear in public unless she is under severe stress. If Melvin is a bright young man who likes to show off his learning, let him use big words like "exacerbate," "bumptious," and "stentorian." (For a comic touch, make it clear that he does not necessarily understand what these words mean.) If Annie is painfully shy, she shouldn't make bold, opinionated declarations such as "This movie is absolutely the biggest piece of trash in the history of Hollywood." She should say instead, "Er—this movie doesn't really have much of a plot, does it?"

If you want to be a skillful writer of dialogue, become aware of how people talk. Go to a restaurant by yourself and listen to the conversation. When you are at school, cock your ear and listen to the voices in the hallway. Learn how children talk, how young adults talk, how senior citizens talk. If you know somebody who is a particularly good conversationalist, listen to him or her carefully. Take note of your friend's most clever remarks. Then try to think of some clever phrases on your own.

Creative Writing — PART THREE: Planning a Story; Dialogue: Listening to the Characters Talk

Date _____   Name _____

ASSIGNMENT: Dialogue and Character

Study the following short speech by a character in a story:

"You don't seem to understand what I mean. Will you please listen to me for once? You're asking me to do something that I think is wrong. Besides, I find you annoying because you talk too much. So kindly go away and stop bothering me."

Rewrite this speech as each of the following characters would say it:

1. An angry eight-year-old _____
_____
_____

2. A super-intellectual with five college degrees _____
_____
_____

3. Shy Annie _____
_____
_____

4. A popular musician _____
_____
_____

5. A clown named Goofus McNutt _____
_____
_____

6. A professional football player named "Buffalo" Brutus _____
_____
_____

Creative Writing

PART THREE: PLANNING A STORY

11. Dialogue: A Few Reminders

Here are some pointers to keep in mind when you are writing dialogue:

1. To make dialogue sound natural, use contractions. Even a learned doctor would probably say, "I'll perform the surgery as soon as I've finished drinking my coffee" instead of "I will perform the surgery as soon as I have finished drinking my coffee."

2. To avoid confusing your readers, start a new paragraph with each change of speaker. You should remember to do this even if you are occasionally left with a one-word paragraph:

"Kristin, hurry up! Are you going to keep me waiting all night?" Heather asked. "Aren't you going to the party?"
"No."
"Why not?"
"Don't ask," said Kristin with a toss of her hair.
Heather stared at her. "But everyone in town will be there."
"Yes, everyone—including that dim-witted, loud mouthed know-it-all, my least favorite lab partner, Mr. Roscoe Sly."

3. Don't worry too much about repeating yourself. It is usually a bad idea to repeat a word carelessly, but when you are writing dialogue, you can use the words "he said" and "she said" as often as necessary. For variety, you might occasionally choose such phrases as "he shouted" and "she whispered," but be careful! Before you know it, your characters will be whimpering, burbling, snorting, hissing, and chortling at the most unlikely times, and your readers will be snickering and sneering.

4. Don't expect adverbs to do your work for you. Here is an example of ineffective dialogue: *"I'm not really very pleased with you," Ralph said angrily.* Well, Ralph may have been angry, but his words show little emotion, and the writer doesn't improve matters by tacking the work "angrily" to the end of the sentence. This is better: *"If I ever see your face again, I'll throw up!" Ralph said.* Adding the word "angrily" to this sentence would be a waste of ink.

5. Use conventional spelling. You will seldom gain anything but confusion by changing the spelling of "was" to "wuz," "your" to "yer," or "dog" to "dawg." If you must use unconventional spelling, use it sparingly. The sentence *"Your dawg was lookin' for you at the school house"* is easy enough to read, but if you write *"Yer dawg wuz lookin' fer ya at th' skool howse,"* most people will have to read the sentence twice in order to understand it.

6. Be careful with slang. You may be tempted to have your characters speak the newest, most up-to-date expressions, but remember that not everyone will know what these words and phrases mean. Besides, slang expressions sometimes vanish from the language in a matter of months, but somebody might want to read your story five years from now. If you want to make your dialogue sound natural without puzzling your readers, use informal words that have been circulating for a

© Mark Twain Media, Inc., Publishers

Creative Writing   PART THREE: Planning a Story; Dialogue: A Few Reminders

long time, such as *mom, fuss, cool,* and *sloppy.* Or, if you really enjoy playing with words, you might try inventing a few brand-new slang expressions of your own. What would it mean to be *gicked over?* If somebody told you that your new clothes look *smarvey* on you, would you feel flattered or insulted? You might have fun making up words—but if you use them in a story, be sure to give some clue as to what the new words mean, like this: "Jane is wearing the most smarvey outfit today! You should see her! She looks exactly like a seasick lizard!"

7. You can use dialogue to introduce background information. For example, suppose you want to let your readers know that Heather's father is a biology teacher and that she has learned something about the scientific method by watching him work. If you want to present this information without being too obvious, you can have Heather say to her uncle, "I used to drop by the high school and help Dad clean up the biology lab after he'd finished teaching for the day. Sometimes it was a yucky job, but I really think it helped me get ready to take science classes."

Date _____ Name _____

ASSIGNMENT: Writing Dialogue

Complete the following conversation in a way that will (a) reveal something important about the two characters and (b) set the scene for a conflict.

    "Hi, Joe," Tanya said. "What's that you've got in your pocket?"
    Joe looked nervous. "What are you talking about?"
    "I just saw you stuff something in your pocket—some sort of paper with red marks on it. Joe, what's the matter with you? All I did was ask—"
    "You must need new glasses or something. How long has it been since you got your eyes checked?"

_____
_____
_____
_____
_____
_____
_____
_____
_____
_____

Creative Writing

PART THREE: PLANNING A STORY

12. Setting: The Scene of the Action

It is important for a writer to pick a suitable *setting,* or location, for his story, a place that is pleasant or scary or depressing or hauntingly beautiful. If the setting is presented convincingly enough, it can almost seem to be a character in the story. Fans of the old television series *Star Trek* will recognize a model of the Starship *Enterprise* almost as quickly as they recognize a picture of Captain Kirk and Mr. Spock. And could anyone imagine *The Wizard of Oz* without the Emerald City, the deadly poppy field, and the state of Kansas? Or *Adventures of Huckleberry Finn* without the Mississippi River? Or *Mary Poppins* without the city of London?

A beginning writer should probably set his stories in the sorts of places that are familiar to him. If you have never traveled to France, don't set your story in Paris—unless you are prepared to read a small mountain of books about Parisian life. Choose the sort of neighborhood, town, or countryside where you have actually lived or visited. But don't try to be completely true to the facts; give your imagination room to work. Perhaps there is a spooky, abandoned house on a corner not far from your home. This deserted building would be the perfect location for a ghost story. But maybe you need a balcony where your ghost can appear, and also a mysterious tower where phantom lights can flicker. If the house on the corner has neither a balcony nor a tower, there is nothing to prevent you from adding both of these features to your imaginary mansion. And maybe you need a place where your characters can retreat occasionally to talk matters over. Why not move your Aunt Gussie's musty antique shop from its present location in Green Bay, Wisconsin, and put it across the street from your haunted house? The best settings are likely to be *fictionalized* descriptions of real places.

If you want to turn your home town into a memorable setting for fiction, concentrate on what makes the place unique or unusual. If you live in a large city, you might describe all of the usual things: skyscrapers pointing to the sky, crowded freeways, gang violence. Or you might focus on something that most people have never thought about before. Perhaps your city has a business that does nothing whatsoever except make, sell, and repair bows for stringed instruments. Or a restaurant that specializes in authentic Scottish food, including the traditional pudding made from the heart and liver of a sheep. If you live in a small town, you could describe dusty roads and cow pastures—or you could build your story around the dingy-looking shop that sells rare tropical fish, or the annual target-shooting competition that draws contestants from around the world, or the house that used to be a station on the Underground Railroad. If you look closely enough, you will find that almost every town has some distinctive feature.

The world has many a place that seems to cry out for a writer to use it as a setting. Think of all the places you have known—beautiful places, ugly places, the places you love, the places you hate, the places that frighten you, the places that seem to beckon. And remember that a "place" can be as small as a window seat or as large as Texas.

© Mark Twain Media, Inc., Publishers

Date_____ Name_____

ASSIGNMENT: Thinking About the Settings of Your Life

1. What places are most familiar to you?
_____
_____
_____

2. What interesting places have you visited?
_____
_____
_____

3. Are there places where you would like to spend more time than you do? Where?
_____
_____
_____

4. Does your hometown have any unusual or interesting features, businesses, or citizens? Describe them.
_____
_____
_____
_____

5. Do you know of a street or geographical feature that has an unusual name (for example, "Old Wire Road," "Deaf Smith County," "Suicide Hill")? Do you know the origins of these names?
_____
_____
_____
_____

6. Is there a place to which you wish never to return? Why?
_____
_____
_____

7. Would any of these places make good settings for stories? Why?
_____
_____
_____

Creative Writing

PART THREE: PLANNING A STORY

13. Writing Effective Description

Good descriptions are brief. Back in the nineteenth century, a writer would sometimes let a description go on for a page or more, but most modern readers have no patience with long descriptive passages and tend to skip over them. Fortunately, it is possible to write a vivid description in only a few sentences. Here is the opening paragraph of Stephen Crane's *The Red Badge of Courage,* a novel about the Civil War:

> *The cold passed reluctantly from the earth, and the retiring fogs revealed an army stretched out on the hills, resting. As the landscape changed from brown to green, the army awakened, and began to tremble with eagerness at the noise of rumors. It cast its eyes upon the roads, which were growing from long troughs of liquid mud to proper thoroughfares. A river, amber-tinted in the shadow of its banks, purled at the army's feet; and at night, when the stream had become of a sorrowful blackness, one could see across it the red, eyelike gleam of hostile camp fires set in the low brows of distant hills.*

Here is another passage from the same novel, describing the scene at a campfire:

> *The fire crackled musically. From it swelled light smoke. Overhead the foliage moved softly. The leaves, with their faces turned toward the blaze, were colored shifting hues of silver, often edged with red. Far off to the right, through a window in the forest could be seen a handful of stars lying, like glittering pebbles, on the black level of night.*

Neither of these passages is long, and neither makes much use of elaborate sentences or four-syllable words. Yet each one does an excellent job of describing a scene and creating a mood. With a little practice, you can write good descriptions too. Here are some things to keep in mind:

1. Appeal to all five senses. One reason why Stephen Crane's descriptions are effective is that they are filled with things to see, hear, and feel. A reader of *The Red Badge of Courage* can see the red-and-silver leaves, hear the murmuring river and the crackling flames, feel the cold morning air and the warmth of the campfire, and smell and taste the rising smoke. (Notice especially how often Crane mentions a specific color.) Any references to one of the senses is called an *image.* Images of sight are probably the most common kind, but every writer should try not to neglect the other four senses. Images of touch can be especially effective. Let your characters shiver with cold, perspire from the heat, feel the softness of a kitten's fur or a spring breeze, scrape their knees against a rough pavement, bask in sunlight, or wade up to their ankles in slimy mud.

2. Focus on what is important or interesting. A good description is specific, but it is seldom wise to mention every detail. If you want to describe Heather, you can say that her height and weight are average, that her hair is black and her eyes are brown, that she is wearing a light blue short-sleeved blouse with the letter "H" stitched on the pocket, that her blue jeans have a patch on the right knee, that she wears an opal ring on the third finger of her left hand, that her shoes . . . but by this time, your readers will have lost interest. You will have buried Heather under a pile of insignificant details. If you want her to make a strong impression, concentrate on two or three of her most striking features: perhaps the keen, purposeful expression in her eyes—eyes that miss nothing—and also the spring in her step, and the silky texture of her hair. Mention the opal ring only if it is to play an important role in the story.

3. Beware of the adjective. Adjectives are the words that describe nouns. They can add a great deal to a description, and for that reason, writers are often tempted to scatter them everywhere. Some writers, in fact, are incapable of writing a noun without immediately adding two or three adjectives: *The stately, shimmering oak tree cast a long, pensive, deepening shadow across the lush, verdant lawn as the rich golden glow of the resplendent summer sunset faded across the silent, silver lake.* But beware: too many adjectives will give your prose a thick, gooey quality. If you are one of those people who find adjectives difficult to resist, you may be able to overcome your temptation by concentrating instead on vivid, action-packed verbs.

4. Avoid qualifiers. In particular, avoid the word "very." In a typical situation, a writer states, "It was a big werewolf" and then decides that the word "big" is not strong enough to describe his monster. So he changes the sentence to "It was a very big werewolf" (or "a pretty big werewolf" or "a rather large werewolf"), and he feels satisfied. Actually, he has added nothing to his description except a useless word. If "big" is not descriptive enough, the writer should try to find a stronger word: he should say that the werewolf was *huge, enormous, massive, as big as a small horse,* or *four feet high at the shoulder.*

ASSIGNMENT: Writing a Description

On your own paper, describe one of your favorite or least favorite places. Include at least one reference to each of the five senses (sight, hearing, touch, smell, taste), and mention at least two specific colors.

Creative Writing

PART THREE: PLANNING A STORY

14. Research Can Be Fun

Here is a scene from *The Phantom of the Community Theatre,* a novel that (let us hope) will never be written: Andy, the hero, has been up all night trying to track down the ghostly figure who is haunting the Safe Harbor Community Theatre. When Andy returns home, he is so exhausted that he collapses on the bench in his mother's azalea garden and sleeps until early evening. He is awakened by the singing of a mockingbird, and he panics when he realizes that he is almost late for his performance as Old Man Pendergast in the Drama Club's latest play. Andy leaps on his bicycle, races along the shore of Lake Michigan as fast as he can pedal, reaches the theatre, and jumps into his clean new costume just as the curtain is about to go up. He is relieved to discover that the costume fits him perfectly. As he starts to make his entrance, his girlfriend, who also has a part in the play, whispers to him, "Good luck."

What's wrong with this scene? Well, for one thing, azaleas and mockingbirds live in warm climates; it would be unusual to find them as far north as Lake Michigan (although Andy might well have been awakened by the screaming of a sea gull). For another thing, unless the Drama Club's director had lost his wits, he would have held at least one dress rehearsal; Andy would not have had to worry about whether his costume would fit. In fact, his costume would probably have been rumpled and stained with grease paint, not fresh and clean. And if Andy were playing the role of an old man, he would not have walked onto the stage without first putting on his makeup. Finally, unless Andy's girlfriend was mad at him and *wanted* him to be kidnapped by the Phantom, she would never have uttered the words "Good luck." Actors believe that these words bring bad luck; they wish one another good luck by saying "Break a leg." The trouble with this story is that the writer did no research.

The old saying "Write about what you know!" is good advice up to a point, especially for beginners. But it would be a dull world if we never learned anything new, and sooner or later, most writers feel the urge to write about something they *don't* know. This is where research comes in. A type of research often done in schools is the *term paper,* which calls for a great deal of reading and careful note-taking. This is one kind of research, but it is not the only kind.

Creative Writing   PART THREE: Planning a Story; Research Can Be Fun

Suppose that you want to write a story in which your heroine is a lifeguard at a public beach. The possibilities are exciting: daring rescues, brushes with death, maybe even a pirate's lost treasure and a shark or two. There's only one problem: you have never been a lifeguard. You haven't the slightest idea how to rescue a drowning person; you don't even swim. Does this mean you have to give up on your story? Not necessarily. Maybe you have a friend who has worked as a lifeguard. You could ask her some questions or arrange to spend a day with her at the beach or the pool. Maybe your local library has a training manual for lifeguards or a good book about water safety. You might even take a few swimming lessons.

The author of *The Phantom of the Community Theatre* could have talked to the high school drama teacher to learn about how plays are produced and how actors talk. He could have checked at the library to find out what birds and plants live near Lake Michigan. He could have spent a day at the local community theatre and tried out for a part, or taken a vacation at Lake Michigan. Writers have many ways of learning information.

A word of warning: most people lead busy lives, so never wait until the last minute to ask a friend or an acquaintance for help with your research. Instead, contact the person several days before your project is due, explain what you are doing, and ask politely whether he or she would be willing to help. Probably the answer will be yes. People usually enjoy talking about their jobs, their hobbies, and their special interests—if they have time.

ASSIGNMENT: Suggestions for Oral Reports

Choose one of the topics below, and do the suggested research. Make an oral report to the class on the information you obtained and any story ideas your research has created.

1. Select a friend or relative who has an interesting job or hobby. Talk to him about his work, his memorable experiences, his daily activities. After the interview, do any story ideas come to your mind?

2. Choose a place where you have never been and would like to go. Read about this place in books, magazine articles, or travel guides, or talk to somebody who has lived there. What kind of story might happen in this place?

3. In your local library, find magazines that were published in the 1960s or earlier. (Old issues of *Look* or *Life* would be good choices.) Study the pictures and advertisements. How did people dress and wear their hair? What products did they buy? What did they worry about? Would you like to have lived in those days?

Creative Writing

PART FOUR: THINKING ABOUT WORDS

15. Build Your Vocabulary

    A writer needs a rich vocabulary, because words are the building blocks of sentences and stories. Words come in many varieties: they can be melodious or harsh, fancy or plain, short or long, gentle or blunt. Some words are elegant; others are so ordinary that they almost get lost on the page; still others grate like the sound of a dentist's drill. Words can be weird, learned, fussy, or simply preposterous. Just as a landscape artist needs paints of many colors, so a writer needs words of many sounds and meanings to tell a good story.

    Obviously, no one—not even a genius like Albert Einstein or Marie Curie—is born with a dictionary in his head. Vocabularies are built gradually over a period of many years. You have already learned a large number of words naturally, just by experiencing life as you grew older. There are no magic tricks to expand your vocabulary overnight, but there are some things you can do that will help speed the process along.

    One of the easiest ways to build your vocabulary is simply to become aware of the words that turn up in the course of your studies. While reading this book, for example, you have already encountered the words *protagonist, antagonist, dialogue,* and *image,* and in later chapters you will find the words *metaphor, thesaurus, tautology,* and *circumlocution.* In history classes you might learn the meanings of such terms as *secede, chivalry, dynasty, veto, jingoism,* and *mugwump.* A study of algebra and geometry will also expand your vocabulary with words like *axiom, diameter, circumference,* and *hypotenuse.* And if you study the art of oil painting you will eventually encounter such jawbreakers as *pointillism* and *chiaroscuro.*

    You can also learn words from sports, hobbies, and other favorite activities. Such pastimes as stamp collecting, ice skating, fishing, cooking, and dancing all have special vocabularies and special terms. What does the word *tackle* mean to a fisherman? To a football player? What do the words *fold* and *whisk* mean to a cook? What is an *axle* to an ice-skater or an *axle* to a mechanic? A *promenade* to a square dancer? Probably the best way to build a colorful vocabulary is to develop many interests and become curious about words.

Books can also help, especially if you read about a variety of subjects. Some people believe that a reader should look up the meaning of every unfamiliar word, but if you are reading for pleasure, you might find it too distracting to be always putting your book down and picking up a dictionary. A better method might be to wait until you see a word that has an interesting look or sound to it. Underline or circle that word so that you can look it up later (or write the word down if you are reading a borrowed book). And if you want the word to linger in your mind, be sure to take note of how the writer used it in a sentence.

If you like to play games, try to become an expert at solving crossword puzzles. Many newspapers publish a crossword puzzle in every issue, and you can also find books of crossword puzzles on the magazine racks. A crossword puzzle dictionary will help you improve your skill. If you prefer board games, get a Scrabble set and enjoy playing this word-building game with your friends or family.

If your parents or your local library subscribes to the magazine *Reader's Digest,* you might try working the "Word Power" exercise in each issue. Or, if you are a good reader and want to learn a large number of new words in a short time, go to the reference section of a bookstore and look for vocabulary-building books. (A popular example is *Thirty Days to a More Powerful Vocabulary* by Wilfred Funk and Norman Lewis.) Or you might start a "word collection" by making lists of words that appeal to you and taping the lists on your mirror or tacking them to your bulletin board. Words are the most inexpensive things you could possibly collect!

ASSIGNMENT: Oral Reports: Vocabulary Building

Work on building your vocabulary by preparing for these oral reports:

1. Find an unfamiliar or peculiar-sounding word in a newspaper, magazine, or book. Look up the word in a dictionary and then tell the class where you found the word and what it means.

2. Choose a hobby, favorite sport, or special interest of yours and make a list of the special words associated with it. Then give a report to the class in which you list some of the most interesting words and explain what they mean.

Creative Writing — PART FOUR: Thinking About Words; Build Your Vocabulary

Date _____   Name _____

ASSIGNMENT: Word Collection

Start your own word collection by looking up the definitions of the following words. Try to use each one in a sentence.

1. procrastinate _____

2. atrocious _____

3. braggadocio _____

4. bumptious _____

5. fiasco _____

6. invective _____

7. debacle _____

8. flaunt _____

9. preen _____

10. carp (as a verb) _____

11. flabbergast _____

12. heinous _____

13. flit _____

14. mellifluous _____

15. dastardly _____

16. effervescent _____

17. scintillating _____

Creative Writing   PART FOUR: Thinking About Words; Build Your Vocabulary

Date _____ Name _____

ASSIGNMENT: Playing with Words

Lewis Carroll, the author of Alice in Wonderland, *liked to invent new words, sometimes by joining two old words together. For example, he combined "flimsy" and "miserable" into "mimsy." He joined "snort" and "chuckle" into "chortle," a word that has become a familiar part of the English language. Carroll called his creations "portmanteau words," after a type of suitcase that opens into two compartments.*

1. Can you invent any portmanteau words of your own?

_____
_____
_____
_____
_____

2. The nonsense poem "Jabberwocky" appears in the first chapter of Lewis Carroll's *Through the Looking Glass.* If you look up the poem and read it, you will find a number of Carroll's made-up words, including *Bandersnatch, uffish,* and *frabjous.* Can you guess what some of these words might mean?

_____
_____
_____
_____
_____

3. Try inventing some words of your own and using them to write a nonsense poem or a brief nonsense story.

_____
_____
_____
_____
_____
_____

Creative Writing

PART FOUR: THINKING ABOUT WORDS

16. The Tools Writers Use

If you were to walk into the office or study of a professional writer, you would probably find a large number of dictionaries and other books on or near the desk (along with a lot of clutter—many writers believe that a tidy desk is the clear sign of an empty mind.) Most writers are smart and some writers are brilliant, but no writer's brain is big enough for all the words, spellings, grammar rules, and guidelines that belong to the English language. A dedicated writer is never too proud to look something up.

The writer's most basic tool is the dictionary. Dictionaries come in many shapes and sizes. The complete or *unabridged* dictionary is probably better suited for a library than for home use. (My unabridged dictionary contains 155,000 words and weighs seven pounds.) A hardback collegiate dictionary, which is smaller and lighter, is a good choice for a household or office bookshelf. But if you want a dictionary that you can really use, get a good paperback edition, which is cheaper, easier to carry, and less clumsy to use than the hardbound versions. A good paperback dictionary might contain about 70,000 words and weigh barely a pound.

A *thesaurus* is a book of synonyms, or words that have similar meanings. One of its purposes is to nudge a word from the back of your mind. Suppose you have written, "Homework is a nuisance." Then you stop to think: homework is worse than a nuisance, but what is it, exactly? You consult a thesaurus and find a list of words: annoyance, pest, botheration, affliction, curse, pestilence, plague . . . *"homework is a plague on the face of the earth!"* At a good bookstore you can find thesauruses for both students and professionals.

Because no two words are exactly alike, a writer may want to own a copy of *Webster's New Dictionary of Synonyms*. This is a special kind of thesaurus that explains the differences among words that mean almost the same thing. What difference does it make, for example, whether you are *intelligent, clever, bright, smart,* or *brilliant?* Webster can tell you.

Many successful authors have published books of advice for beginning writers. If you have found this book useful, you might also enjoy reading a work by Sandy Asher entitled *Where Do You Get Your Ideas?* This lively little book is filled with suggestions for writing both prose and poetry, as well as words of wisdom from a number of famous writers. Asher has also written a book entitled *Wild Words! How to Train Them to Tell Stories.*

A poet will probably keep a rhyming dictionary close at hand, in case he needs to know whether any words rhyme with *dinosaur, historical,* or *highwayman.* A journalist might have more use for a book of usage. For example, a critic reviewing a concert might write, "A large amount of people attended the program." Then she might pause, chew her pen, cross out the word "amount," and write "number." Which word is correct? Our critic can find the answer in a book like *The Careful Writer* by Theodore Bernstein. (The answer: the word *number* refers to things that can be counted, and it is possible to count the people at a concert. Use *amount* for substances that can't be counted, as in "The Midwest received a large amount of rainfall in the spring of 1993.")

Handbooks for grammar and usage come in all sizes, shapes, and levels of difficulty. (One of the most unusual of these books is entitled *The Transitive Vampire,* but this is not an especially good choice for beginners.) Sooner or later, every serious writer will have to read *The Elements of Style* by William Strunk and E. B. White. Perhaps you will remember E. B. White as the author of *Charlotte's Web,* a masterpiece of children's literature. *The Elements of Style* is also a masterpiece, and it is short—less than a hundred small pages.

Creative Writing PART FOUR: Thinking About Words; The Tools Writers Use

If the writer is serious about getting his work published, he will also need a subscription to at least one magazine. *The Writer* and *Writer's Digest* are two of the top choices. Many writers also read *Publishers Weekly,* which contains the latest news about the practical world of publishing. *Writer's Market,* published in book form once a year, lists the names and addresses of book publishers, magazine editors, and agents.

Every writer, whether he or she is a student or a professional, must have some kind of handbook. If the writer is really working hard, that book will eventually grow ragged from use. These days, a writer may get some help from his computer, because a modern word-processing program may include a built-in spelling checker, thesaurus, and guide to grammar. But the writer had better wait for a few years before he throws away his dictionary and thesaurus. The computer's memory is not yet powerful enough to answer all questions, so it never hurts to have a few books lying around, just in case.

Date _____ Name _____

ASSIGNMENT: Special Projects: A Writer's Tools

1. Go to the reference section of a bookstore or library. If necessary, ask the clerk or librarian to help you find the reference books for writers. Examine some of the books. Which ones might be useful to you?

_____
_____
_____
_____

2. If you can find a rhyming dictionary, consult it to find out how many words rhyme with *trail.* Can you write the words to a song about a cowboy riding along a trail?

_____
_____
_____
_____
_____
_____
_____
_____
_____
_____

Creative Writing

PART FOUR: THINKING ABOUT WORDS

17. Be Brief!

"Brevity is the soul of wit," wrote William Shakespeare, and he was right. Nobody enjoys wading through pages of tedious and pointless writing. Even the best joke would lose its sparkle if we had to listen to fifteen minutes of boring chatter in order to hear the punch line. So it is important for a writer to learn which words are necessary and which can be cut, because useless words can pile up faster than one realizes.

A useless word is one that serves no purpose except to take up space on the page. It adds nothing to a description; it contains no interesting information; it is flat, colorless, and lifeless. A writer creates beauty and excitement with vivid words, but he can do without the useless ones.

You have already learned to avoid the passive voice whenever possible. Passive verbs are not only tame but also wordy: *Andy kicked the football* is two words shorter than *The football was kicked by Andy.* In particular, avoid using two passive verbs in one sentence: *It is believed by many that football is considered to be an exciting sport.* Get rid of those passive verbs and write simply *Football is an exciting sport.*

Keep your eye out, too, for expressions and phrases that are longer than they need to be. Consider this sentence: *Because of the fact that I overslept for too long, I arrived at class in a tardy manner.* You can express this idea much more briefly: *Because I overslept, I was late to class.* Instead of writing *Scrooge often reacted to others in ways that expressed great anger,* you can write instead, *Scrooge had a terrible temper.*

A special kind of wordiness is the *tautology* (taw-TAH-luh-jee), in which an idea is needlessly repeated. If the editor of a newspaper were having a bad day, he might write something like this: *The true fact is that because of our leaking water tower, this community is faced with a serious emergency, and we must take immediate action in the near future.* No doubt the editor means well, but did you ever hear of an emergency that *wasn't* serious? Can there be such a thing as a false fact? And when else can one take immediate action except in the near future? The editor might make a better impression on his readers if he would simply write *This community must repair its leaking water tower immediately.*

A *circumlocution* (sir-cum-loh-CYU-shun) is a way of using big words and lengthy phrases to "talk around" a subject. Some serious writers use circumlocutions in an effort to sound intelligent and well educated. For such people, a simple classroom becomes a "learning environment," and a report card might be an "evaluation instrument." A circumlocution expert will always "form relationships" instead of making friends, and he never explains if he can "articulate." Instead of "the farmer's plow," he says, "the agriculturist's soil cultivation implement."

Such language has its uses, but there is no special magic about a big word just because it is big. Four- and five-syllable words may be fun to play with, but a skillful writer will use a long word only when he really needs it. For most purposes, "farmer" is a better word than "agriculturist," and "classroom" makes more sense than "learning enviornment."

Creative Writing PART FOUR: Thinking About Words; Be Brief!

Date _____ Name _____

ASSIGNMENT: Thinking About Brevity

Rewrite the following sentences to make them more brief and forceful:

1. Because there was a definite possibility that the officers of the law might be patrolling the area, I manipulated my automobile in a careful manner.

2. "This puzzling mystery cannot be solved quickly overnight," uttered the detective in a voice that had the quality of a whisper.

3. It is believed by many that a canine companion is the most reliable supportive relationship known to *Homo sapiens*.

4. If an education professional desires to enjoy satisfactory relationships with the younger generation, it is necessary to make use of the honest method of communication.

5. Mighty Casey made a rapid ambulatory motion in the direction of home plate.

6. At this point in time, I am seriously and earnestly considering the idea of asking Dorothy whether she would agree to enter into a matrimonial arrangement with me.

Write an "intellectual" version of a well-known song, familiar quotation, or verse from the Bible.

Creative Writing

PART FOUR: THINKING ABOUT WORDS

18. How To Use Figures of Speech

Almost everyone enjoys imaginative language. For people who work with language—poets, song writers, ministers, journalists, storytellers of all sorts—*figures of speech* are among the most useful tricks of the trade. Figures of speech come in many varieties (about 250 types, to be more exact), but the most common of them involve some kind of comparison between things that are basically different.

Probably the simplest figure of speech is the *simile* (SIM-uh-lee), a direct comparison almost always making use of the word *like* or *as.* For example, a person who is feeling wretched with the flu might say, "My throat feels like a dry cactus, and my head is as heavy as a block of cement." Notice that our flu sufferer is not exactly telling the truth: a sore throat does not really resemble a cactus, and a stopped-up head is nothing like a cement block. Nevertheless, the similes make this description more vivid than if the patient had simply said, "I have a scratchy throat and a clogged nose." Often a familiar English expression will take the form of a simile (weak as a kitten, sharp as a tack, multiply like rabbits, fast as the wind, March comes in like a lion and goes out like a lamb). Such an expression is called a *cliché,* a figure of speech that has been worn out with overuse. Good writers try to avoid clichés as often as possible.

A *metaphor* (MET-uh-for), like the simile, is a comparison of two unlike things, but the comparison is implied rather than directly stated. Our flu patient would be speaking metaphorically if he said "I have a cactus in my throat and cement in my nose." In Shakespeare's play *Romeo and Juliet,* Romeo praises the woman he loves by saying, "Juliet is the sun." He might also have used a simile and said, "Juliet is as radiant as the sun." But Romeo, like a good many writers, apparently believed that the metaphor is more forceful than the simile. Notice also that in the examples given above, the metaphor uses fewer words than the simile.

A *personification* occurs when a writer describes a thing or a force of nature as if it were human, as in *The cruel flood waters swept across the farm while the sorrowful wind sighed in pity.* Everyone knows, of course, that water feels no ill will, nor can the wind sympathize. But a person who has lived through a flood might find a certain poetic truth in these figures of speech.

Somewhat similar to the personification is the *apostrophe,* a favorite of poets, who often like to address a force of nature as if it could understand human language. A famous example is a line by the English poet Byron: "Roll on, thou deep and dark blue ocean, roll!"

Figures of speech are so much fun to invent that you may be tempted to use them helter-skelter. But you should resist this temptation, especially when you are writing prose. Figures of speech are the salt and pepper of language. Used sparingly, salt and pepper can enhance the flavor of good food; used excessively, they can ruin an otherwise tasty meal.

Also, beware of the so-called *mixed metaphor.* In other words, don't make two comparisons at once, as in this sentence: *After the party, our living room looked as if it had been buried under a tidal wave of confusion.* The problem is that tidal waves don't bury objects; they sweep objects away. The sentence should be revised to read "swept by a tidal wave" or "buried under an avalanche."

Creative Writing PART FOUR: Thinking About Words; How to Use Figures of Speech

Date _____ Name _____

ASSIGNMENT: Figures of Speech

Complete the following similes, trying to avoid clichés:

1. After I ate the spoiled hot dogs, I was as sick as _____

2. The werewolf was as angry as _____

3. My collie is as gentle as _____

4. The party was as much fun as _____

5. A good book is like _____

6. This tight shoe hurts as if _____

7. The movie was as dull as _____

8. After the mud volleyball tournament, I was as dirty as _____

Write a letter to the wind, the rain, an ocean, a lake, or some other force of nature.

Try to think of an appropriate metaphor for each of the following:

1. Homework (example: Homework is a dirty dish that has to be scrubbed for an hour every night.)
   _____

2. A loyal friend _____

3. A dentist _____

4. A rainy Monday morning _____

5. A bright Friday afternoon _____

6. A stray dog _____

7. A large spider _____

© Mark Twain Media, Inc., Publishers

Creative Writing

PART FOUR: THINKING ABOUT WORDS

19. Diction: Words That Say What You Mean

One of a writer's most important tasks is to get the right word in the right place. Words are fun, but they are also tricky, and some words can be dangerous if they are used incorrectly. So it is important to be alert to the meaning of words and to follow a simple rule: *When in doubt, consult your dictionary.*

It is generally a bad idea to use a word if you are uncertain about its meaning, because some words present a misleading appearance. A good example is *fulsome,* which looks as if it might mean "full" or "complete." But if you should try to compliment one of your friends on his "fulsome report" to the members of the Hockey Club, be prepared for him to throw a puck at you. The word *fulsome* actually means "offensively insincere."

One of the most famous characters in English literature is Mrs. Malaprop, who appears in an eighteenth century play entitled *The Rivals* by Richard Brinsley Sheridan. Mrs. Malaprop loves to use big words, but she rarely knows exactly what they mean. To this day, the word *malapropism* refers to a confusion of words that sound similar but mean entirely different things. Imagine a bumbling detective who has a flair for malapropisms—a character like Constable Dogberry in Shakespeare's play *Much Ado About Nothing.* A modern Dogberry might tell his supervisor that he spotted an *auspicious* character lurking around the scene of a jewel robbery, that he has *comprehended* this individual, and that he has solved the crime and will clear up any remaining *contusion* by issuing a *lurid* report. The detective is confusing *auspicious* (favorable) with *suspicious* and *comprehend* (to understand) with *apprehend* (to arrest). When he uses the word *contusion* (a bruise), he is trying for *confusion,* and he intends for his report to be *lucid* (clear) rather than *lurid* (gruesome).

To avoid sounding like Mrs. Malaprop and Constable Dogberry, check your dictionary. You should also remember that no two words mean exactly the same thing. Even though words may be listed as synonyms in a dictionary or thesaurus, you can't necessarily use them interchangeably. Some dictionaries list *famous* and *notorious* as synonyms, but if you are given the assignment of introducing an Olympic goalie at a meeting of the Hockey Club, it would be foolhardy to describe him as "one of the most notorious athletes in the world." The word *notorious* is usually applied to such rascals as bank robbers, swindlers, and assassins—people who are famous for their bad deeds, not their service to mankind.

Every writer should strive for vivid language, but in the age of television, it is easy to be tempted by words that are too powerful or too forceful to describe an ordinary event. In television commercials, every bargain is *spectacular,* every bowl of soup explodes with *sensational* flavor, and every mousetrap is the most *fabulous* one ever built. Such language may be fine for advertising, but you should avoid using it in ordinary writing. Think twice before writing, "The musicians ended their concert with a spectacular love song." That love song might have been sweet, sad, tender, lilting, haunting, or even beautiful, but it could be spectacular only if it were performed by an eighty-piece orchestra, accompanied by fireworks and a laser light show.

On the other hand, some words are so tame that they mean almost nothing. A good example is the word *fun,* as in "Annette had fun during her trip to Chicago." What does this sentence actually tell us? Some people think it's fun to go to the opera; others hate opera and would rather go to a wrestling match; still others would prefer an afternoon at the library or the museum; and some people's idea of fun is to sleep all afternoon. Exactly what did Annette do in Chicago? We will never

© Mark Twain Media, Inc., Publishers

Creative Writing PART FOUR: Thinking About Words; Diction: Words That Say What You Mean

know unless the writer tells us: "Annette saw the dolphin show at the oceanarium and then cheered herself hoarse at a baseball game."

Other tame words are *nice, interesting, neat, thing,* and *stuff* ("Annette had a nice time in Chicago and saw a lot of interesting things. She went shopping and bought some neat stuff.") Use these words sparingly, if at all; concentrate instead on words that say what you mean.

Date _____ Name _____

ASSIGNMENT: Thinking About Diction

1. What is wrong with the following paragraph?

I really enjoyed our family vacation at the Wild and Wicked West Theme Park. The park is full of interesting rides and a lot of other fun things to do. The ice cream shop is awesome, and some of the other stores are out of this world. The park is educational, too. I learned a lot about America's past at some of the hysterical exhibits. We saw a lot of good shows, and when I listened to the patriotic music, I became conscience of a deep pride in my country. Everybody should go to the Wild and Wicked West because it's a good place to spend a vacation.

Try to write a better description of the Wild and Wicked West Theme Park.

_____
_____
_____
_____
_____
_____
_____
_____
_____
_____
_____

2. By now you should have some ideas about how to write well—but you should also be an expert on how to write badly. Using your own paper, write the first page of the worst book, story, or article in the world. Use passive verbs, mix your metaphors, repeat yourself, talk all around the subject, and clutter your page with unnecessary words. Your work can be either fiction or non-fiction—the only requirement is that it be really awful!

Creative Writing

PART FIVE: IMAGINATION

20. Let Your Mind Soar!

The word *imagination* means many things. For example, if we say that a book is a work of "imaginative literature," we are implying that the book is fiction rather than nonfiction and possibly that it deals with fantasy rather than real life. If we say that six-year-old Yvonne has "a lively imagination," this means that she can keep a perfectly earnest face while she tells a story about her pet unicorn and her kindly old grandmother who happens to be a witch. If we say that a particular student is good at finding "imaginative solutions to problems," we mean that he looks beyond what is obvious: he sees similarities in things that appear to be different and differences in things that appear to be similar. He would find it easy to write a ten-page paper on the topic "Explain why a professional football player is like a babysitter." If he is asked to write about George Washington, he does more than look up the facts and figures; he brings Washington to the twentieth century on a time machine. If a student is truly imaginative, he might even be able to answer Lewis Carroll's famous riddle, "Why is a raven like a writing-desk?"

Imagination is one of the most important qualities for a writer to have—or any artist, for that matter. Through imagination, the artist can enter into the mind of another person and view the world through different eyes. He can take bits and pieces of his knowledge and own experience and combine them to form something completely new: a story, a play, a ballet, or the script for a movie. Or he can travel to places that never existed: Neverland, the Emerald City of Oz, Middle Earth, Alice's Wonderland, or the strange and distant planets of Madeline L'Engle's *A Wrinkle in Time*.

Often an imaginative story begins with a "what-if" question. What if magic really worked? What if spell-casting were a science rather than a fantasy? Consider the possibilities. If magic were real, the schools would probably have spell-casting competitions in which students tried to dazzle the judges with their skills. Chances are, there would be at least one contestant who was all dazzle and no substance: he could create an impressive amount of smoke and brilliant lightning flashes, but he could pull no rabbits out of hats, nor could he make a piece of pie disappear except by eating it. Still the judges might be fooled by his act and give him the gold medal. There might also be one contestant who had impressive talents but no money to pay her tuition to the Academy of Sorcery—and talent is often useless unless it is trained. She might get a scholarship if she could win the contest—but suppose she is a serious magician who is not especially good at light-and-smoke shows? Will the judges recognize true ability when they see it? When such ideas begin stirring in your mind, you are not far from a story about the young magician's uphill struggle to become a full-fledged sorcerer.

What if you could fly? What a happy thought!—no more trudging around by foot, no more waiting on buses or begging people to drive you to your destinations; you would simply launch yourself into the air. No more fear of the school bully: if you saw him coming, you would simply fly away. And think of the fun you could have swooping through clouds and turning aerial somersaults over church steeples! But what would be the drawbacks? Well, people would start to wonder why you always looked as if you had just stepped in out of a hurricane. And if anyone found out about your special ability, you would quickly be surrounded by hordes of reporters and tourists who would not give you a minute's peace. And what if you turned out to be especially susceptible to airsickness? You might yearn for your old earthbound life!

If you dream of writing fantasy, science fiction, or weird tales of the supernatural, let your imagination fly free. You'll find it easy to think of ideas if you remember to ask the question "What if?"

© Mark Twain Media, Inc., Publishers

Creative Writing   PART FIVE: Imagination; Let Your Mind Soar!

Date _____ Name _____

ASSIGNMENT: Considering the "What-Ifs"

To stimulate your imagination, try to answer some of the following questions:

1. What if you could travel through time? _____
_____
_____

2. What if a strange man or woman came to your home and offered you a single wish?
_____
_____

3. What if an alien spaceship landed in your back yard? _____
_____
_____

4. What if Superman rented the upstairs rooms in your house or the apartment next to yours?
_____
_____

5. What if ghosts were real? _____
_____
_____

6. What if you had a personal robot or a dog or cat that was more intelligent than most people are?
_____
_____

7. What if you lived in a country where music was forbidden?
_____
_____

8. What if you had a dream one night and awoke the next morning to find that your dream had come true?
_____
_____
_____

© Mark Twain Media, Inc., Publishers

Creative Writing

PART FIVE: IMAGINATION

21. Don't *Be Yourself!*

Have you ever had to start classes at a new school or attend a party where almost everyone was a stranger to you? If so, perhaps your friends and relatives tried to calm your feelings of nervousness by saying, "Oh, just relax and be yourself." No doubt their advice was good, but if you are a writer, you might find it far more exciting *not* to be yourself, to enter imaginatively into the life and mind of another person, an animal, an intelligent machine, or a supernatural creature. Using your imagination will not only make you a better writer but will also broaden your understanding of other people and help you to sympathize with them more fully.

If you want to write about a prince, try to get inside his skin, think his thoughts, see the world through his eyes. Use your imagination to transform yourself into the prince. Do you have a good life? Yes, in some respects. You have a stable full of fine horses, ten closets full of clothes, an entire room full of computers and compact discs, and your own car and chauffeur. But you don't see much of your parents (the King and Queen) because they spend their time making speeches, opening supermarkets, and giving banquets for visiting heads of state. You are being raised by a succession of nannies—and what if one of them turns out to be cruel and dislikes you? To whom can you turn for help? Who will feel sorry for you? After all, princes aren't supposed to have problems!

But suppose you survive your problems with nannies. One day you reach the age of fourteen or fifteen, and suddenly you are yanked out of the royal palace and packed off to boarding school. You find yourself living in a barn-like dormitory with a hundred other boys—you, a prince who has never had to make his own bed before. Although your fellow students treat you with respect, they look upon you as a spoiled brat. Several months pass, and you have yet to make a single real friend. You give a speech at assembly, and it's a good speech, but nobody takes you seriously, because you are the prince—a relic of the Middle Ages. You try out for the choir, and you give the best audition, but the choir director doesn't want to be accused of favoritism, so he gives the solo part to another boy. Then you get caught pouring flour into the choir director's hat. It's a harmless prank, but the headmaster doesn't want to be accused of "going easy" on the prince, so he throws the book at you: you are suspended from the choir and confined to your room on weekends for the rest of the term. It all seems unfair, but you don't dare complain, because princes are supposed to be brave. Besides, who would listen to you?

© Mark Twain Media, Inc., Publishers

Creative Writing PART FIVE: Imagination; *Don't* Be Yourself!

When you eavesdrop on the conversations of your schoolmates, you discover that all of them have more freedom than you do. They can go to town without taking their bodyguards along. They can choose to be doctors and lawyers and astronauts when they grow up, but you have no choice; your career was decided at the moment you were conceived. You really want to be a good prince—and a good king someday—but you would like to make a few decisions for yourself, and you wish that everyone would quit treating you like a freak. What will you do—what *can* you do—to win the respect of your classmates, your teachers, and your future subjects?

If you don't like being a prince, try being a dog. Dogs have weak eyesight but a keen sense of smell. How would it feel to perceive the world with your nose instead of your eyes? If you were a dog, what kind of poetry would you write? How would you compliment your doggy girlfriend or boyfriend? As a dog, you would probably divide your time between eating, sleeping, lying in the sun, playing with small children, chasing rabbits, and getting your fur stroked—a good life indeed, unless you got kidnapped and imprisoned in a scientific laboratory to be used as the subject of a diabolical experiment. Then you would be in a real fix! How would you escape? And once you escaped, how would you inform the police about your captors and their evil plans? You certainly wouldn't be able to pick up the telephone and call the local police station!

Maybe you would rather be yourself. But remember, your writing life will be more exciting if you ignore the usual wise advice. Be yourself at parties, but when you sit down to write, *don't be yourself!*

ASSIGNMENT: Identifying with a Fictional Character

1. Write an essay from the viewpoint of the fictional prince described in this chapter. Describe how you feel about your situation, and explain what you plan to do that will improve your life.

2. Write an essay about how it would feel to be one of the following characters:

- A homeless cat
- A dolphin who lives in the ocean (but who might get captured and taken to an oceanarium or theme park)
- A happy hobo
- A robot (*you* decide what kind of robot)
- A monkey in a zoo
- An explorer on a distant planet
- A cowboy in the old West
- A turtle trying to cross a crowded freeway

Creative Writing

PART FIVE: IMAGINATION

22. A New World

If you enjoy creating fictitious characters, you might also like the challenge of creating an imaginary city or town. Think of street names, prominent citizens, interesting geographical features, names for schools. Is there an ocean, a lake, or a river nearby? Does a creek run through the city park? Is this park a safe place for walking after dark? Why or why not? What kinds of stores are located in the business district? How does the average citizen earn his or her living? Is this town a good place to live, or is it a place where everyone dreams of escape? Like people, most towns and cities have personalities of their own.

But there's no need for you to be satisfied with creating a mere city. Why not an entire country, a world, or even a whole new *universe* of your own? The fields of science fiction and fantasy offer numerous possibilities: far-away planets and galaxies, time travel (both forward and backward), journeys through the looking glass or into black holes, utopian societies and nightmarish dictatorships, parallel time frames, and even alternate universes. In creating your own world, the problem is to make it believable and consistent. You will have to work out the details carefully, because your world will have to be fairly complex in order to be convincing.

Let us suppose, for example, that you want to create an earth-like planet with an important difference: mermaids and mermen really exist. They live in the oceans, where they form "schools," as fish do. They elect leaders, recount legends, play a variety of watery games, and perform elaborate water ballets. Once in a great while, one of them grows adventurous enough to crawl up onto dry land. Meanwhile, the men and women on the shore carry on their typical human activities: building cities, planting farms, carrying on businesses, writing books—and, occasionally, fighting wars.

What would such a world be like? Consider the details. What do mermaids and mermen eat? What would their Olympic Games be like? What jewelry would they wear? How would their fashions come and go? By what titles would they address their leaders, and how would they hold elections? What do a merman and his bride say to each other during the wedding ceremony? What would be a prize insult for a merman? ("You're as useless as an octopus with one tentacle"? "You don't have enough energy to make a good sponge"?)

And what happens when the mer-folk encounter human beings? Almost certainly there would be suspicion and distrust on both sides. The mer-folk might view the humans as soft and helpless: most of them can't swim more than a few yards without getting tired; they need clumsy boats to carry them across the ocean; they're always getting themselves into trouble and having to be rescued from drowning; they can't even understand the language the dolphins speak! And yet, for all their weaknesses, look how conceited they are, imagining themselves to be the lords of creation! The human beings, on the other hand, might view the mer-folk as mere "fish people," ignorant, backward, unable to read and write (it is difficult to print or store books in the water). Eventually, some sort of embassy would have to be created to settle differences between the two sides. But suppose the daughter of the mer-folk ambassador should go to a party at the embassy, where she happens to meet the son of a human senator? And suppose the two of them were immediately attracted to each other?

Try using your imagination, and you will find that it's fun to visit a new city, world, or universe.

Creative Writing PART FIVE: Imagination; A New World

Date _____ Name _____

ASSIGNMENT: A World of Your Own

1. Think of a name for an imaginary planet: _____

2. This world is similar to Earth, but with one important difference. What is different? (Do intelligent robots exist? Do real elves and goblins live in the woods? Do vampires roam the city streets after dark? Is there a giant space station hovering overhead?)

_____

_____

3. How is the average person's life affected by this difference?

_____

_____

4. What subjects are taught in the schools that would not be taught on Earth?

_____

_____

_____

5. How is political life different?

_____

_____

6. What sorts of books might be written on this planet?

_____

_____

_____

7. If you lived on this planet, what would you do?

_____

_____

_____

_____

© Mark Twain Media, Inc., Publishers

Creative Writing

PART FIVE: IMAGINATION

23. Let's Make a Deal—Now!

Thirty years ago, scholars and thinkers had a wonderful time predicting what life in the future would be like. Many of them envisioned a dazzling new world: glittering cities with moving sidewalks to make life easy for shoppers, colonies on the moon, explorers walking on the ocean's floor, a private helicopter for everyone. A visitor to the New York World's Fair could see this vision brought to life in dazzling exhibits reminiscent of Disney World. But surely the most remarkable thing about this vision is that the prophets got everything wrong.

It turned out that most people didn't want the glistening cities; they preferred leafy suburbs. They didn't want moving sidewalks (except in airports); they wanted enclosed malls where they could shop without getting rained on. They didn't want to build cities on the moon or take walks on the floor of the ocean; they wanted devices to make life more pleasant and convenient right here on solid Earth: microwave ovens that could cook a meal in minutes, computers small enough to sit on a desk, video players to bring uncut full-length movies into their homes.

For a writer of imaginative fiction, the lesson is clear: when you try to look into the future, your crystal ball will be cloudy unless you think not of possibilities but of *people*. Instead of asking, "What technology is possible?" ask "What do people need? What do they want and enjoy? What are their fondest dreams, their worst nightmares?" A writer should also remember that where technology is concerned, sometimes the little things are the most important. Today we think of the telephone as a simple, normal device, but it has probably had more of an effect on our lives than the Apollo moon landings did. And all of our lives continue to be transformed every day by computers that are no bigger than bread boxes.

Try to look into the future. What gadget would make your life happier and easier? How about a self-cleaning bathtub? A "garbage chute" that would whisk your trash into the city incinerator, eliminating the need for you to lug the smelly stuff to the curb? A boat that could also travel on land? A light bulb that never needs to be changed? (Unfortunately, this invention would mean the end of the light bulb joke.)

Would you like to have a universal book? Let's say you are strolling along the banks of the Mississippi River and you take a sudden notion to read a book by Mark Twain. Your universal book looks like a pocket-sized computer. You whip it out of your pocket, punch in the letters M-A-R-K T-W-A-I-N, and settle down to read the text of *Life on the Mississippi* or *Huckleberry Finn,* which is beamed by satellite onto your mini-screen.

Are you bored by the monotony of green grass? Would you like to plant your lawn with genetically engineered grass that could grow in shades of red, yellow, flamingo pink, turquoise blue, or any color you wanted? Planted in patterns, the blades of colored grass could form pictures of stars, flowers, bears, or the signing of the Declaration of Independence. (A drawback might be that your neighbor could sue you if he decided that your purple-and-pink lawn clashed with his orange and blue one.)

So use your imagination and enjoy gazing into the future. Plenty of gadgets, gizmos, and contraptions are still waiting to be invented!

Creative Writing PART FIVE: Imagination; Let's Make a Deal—Now!

Date _____ Name _____

ASSIGNMENT: Oral Report: Let's Make a Deal—Now!

1. Imagine a futuristic invention that many people might find useful or entertaining. Describe it.
_____
_____
_____

2. Think of a name for this device. _____

3. Write a list of reasons why everyone should have this device in his or her home.
_____
_____
_____
_____

4. Write a script for a television-style commercial in which you will try to "sell" your invention. Then present the commercial to your class. If you like, you may ask one or two of your classmates to participate. Feel free to use charts, graphs, posters, props, tape recordings, or any other audio-visual device.
_____
_____
_____
_____
_____
_____
_____
_____
_____
_____
_____

Creative Writing

PART FIVE: IMAGINATION

24. Tall Tales

Americans love to exaggerate. Perhaps this is because ours is a big country, with wide prairies, towering mountains, sprawling cities, dense forests, and severe weather. Exaggeration would come naturally to people who live in such a place. Also, we are proud of our ancestors and their heroic struggles to settle the wilderness. We love to tell stories about them, and somehow these stories always seem to get better with the passing of time.

A favorite type of American humor is the *tall tale,* which is often a story about the wild and amazing adventures of an impossible hero. Most Americans are familiar with the exploits of such characters as Davy Crockett, Daniel Boone, Johnny Appleseed, Pecos Bill, and Paul Bunyan. Tall tales were often set on the American frontier. The typical tall tale hero weighed forty pounds at birth and killed his first mountain lion at the age of two. He was raised by a grizzly bear and grew to be twenty feet tall. He became the greatest hunter, cowboy, sailor, fireman, soldier, or pioneer in all history. In his spare time, he captured bolts of lightning and tamed them until they were as gentle as house cats. He rode a horse that was big enough to drink rivers dry.

Tall tales often dealt with an occupation of some sort. Pecos Bill was a cowboy, Paul Bunyan was a lumberman, John Henry worked on the railroad, Mike Fink was a boatman, and a character named "Mose" was a fireman in New York City. When a tall tale hero was hard at work, his deeds could be astounding. Pecos Bill, for example, once ended a drought by lassoing a tornado and riding it, just as a cowboy rides a bucking horse, until the storm became exhausted and rained itself to death. (Bill's lasso was about as long as the equator.) When Paul Bunyan needed water to float logs, he single-handedly dug the Columbia River.

Wonderful as these heroes were, you probably would not want them as your neighbors, because they had more energy than they knew what to do with, and as a result, they often got into fights. Besides, they were constantly bragging about themselves and their talents. A bragging champion was called a "ring-tailed roarer." If he wanted to convince everyone that he was the meanest man on earth, he would leap into the air, let out a loud whoop, and say something like: "Look at me! My father was a blizzard, my mother was a volcano, my great-aunt was a tidal wave, and the forest fires are my cousins! Destruction is my middle name! I eat ten wolves for breakfast every morning and then use pine trees for toothpicks!"

Oddly enough, the very qualities that made a hero great might also make it impossible for him to live a normal life. For this reason, there was often a touch of sadness in the tall tale. The hero was a lonely man: if somebody moved to within ten miles of his place, he began feeling crowded and had to move on. Sometimes his wonderful career came to an end when he met a machine that could do the job better than he could. Mike Fink quit his boating job and headed west when the steamboat was invented. John Henry won a contest with a steam drill, but the intense effort killed him. In some versions of the Pecos Bill story, Bill's spirit was broken when he lost his sweetheart, a woman named Sue.

If you would like to try writing a tall tale of your own, you should use a *deadpan* style. That is, you should tell your story in a matter-of-fact way, as if it were perfectly normal to ride on a tornado or dig a river bare-handed. Much of the humor of the tall tales comes from this deadpan style. The events of your story should be larger than life and maybe even preposterous, but you should tell the story as if it were so obviously true that no one could doubt your honesty for a single minute.

© Mark Twain Media, Inc., Publishers

Creative Writing   PART FIVE: Imagination; Tall Tales

Date _____   Name _____

ASSIGNMENT: The Tall Tale

1. The frontier tale usually dealt with some kind of job or occupation. Can you think of any modern occupations where a tall tale hero might find work?

_____
_____
_____
_____

2. The heroes of the tall tales were usually men, although a hero would sometimes have a wife who was as extraordinary as he was. Could a tall tale be told about a woman? What sort of woman might make a good heroine for a tall tale?

_____
_____
_____
_____

3. Can you think of qualities that might seem admirable in a hero but not so admirable in an ordinary person? What are the advantages and disadvantages of being highly energetic?

_____
_____
_____
_____

4. Can you think of any well-known movie characters who resemble the heroes of tall tales? Name a few.

_____
_____
_____
_____

Try spinning a tall tale of your own. You can set your story either in the past or in the modern age.

© Mark Twain Media, Inc., Publishers

Creative Writing

PART SIX: WRITING YOUR STORY

25. Writing and Revising

Now that you have learned how to use words, build a plot, and create good characters, it's time to think seriously about writing a story of your own.

Many writers begin their work on a story by jotting down a first version called a *rough draft* or *first draft.* Later they will either make corrections or rewrite the entire story in a more thoughtful, leisurely manner. But writers work in many different ways. Some people can produce a perfectly good story in only one draft; others are not happy until they have rewritten everything nine or ten times. Some writers wouldn't even think about beginning work on a story until they have made a bubble chart of ideas and written an outline of the plot and a biography of each main character. Others just plunge right in. Some writers set their alarm clocks for five in the morning; others do their best work late at night. And some writers demand absolute peace and quiet, while others do their best writing at a booth in a crowded, noisy restaurant.

Part of your job as a writer is to discover what works best for you. Are you more alert in the morning or in the afternoon? How many drafts do you have to make in order to feel satisfied with your manuscript? Can you work better if you listen to music? Do you need to make an outline or otherwise plan ahead before you start to write? Only you can answer these questions. Be suspicious of anyone who tells you that there is only one way to write.

Almost everyone agrees on one thing, however: if you want to be a successful writer who finishes work on time, *you must have a schedule.* This is why it is important for you to determine your best hours of the day. For a student writer, a good plan would be to reserve three or four hours during the week as your "writing time"—the hour immediately after classes on Mondays, Wednesdays, and Fridays, for example; or the hour before classes if you're an early-morning person; or half an hour after supper Monday through Thursday and another hour on Sunday afternoon. The only requirement is that your schedule work for you.

As a beginner, you should probably get in the habit of making an outline before you get down to serious work on a writing project. This outline need not be highly elaborate (if your outline is longer than you expect the story to be, you'll know you've overdone it), but it should serve as a kind of road map so that you will know exactly where your story is going and how it will reach its conclusion. You should also plan on making at least two drafts: a first draft to capture your ideas on paper and a second draft to eliminate mistakes, improve descriptions, and generally polish your work. Don't sit hunched over your writing desk until your mind is exhausted. After you have finished your rough draft, put it away for a day or two, so that your mind will be fresh when you write the second version. (Your mind can get tired just as your body can.) If you don't feel happy with your first draft, *don't worry—your feelings are perfectly normal!* Remember that you can always make changes in the second draft.

© Mark Twain Media, Inc., Publishers

Creative Writing   PART SIX: Writing Your Story; Writing and Revising

Date _____   Name _____

ASSIGNMENT: Outlining

Read the following short story and take note of the various complications in the plot. Then try making a short outline of the story. What sort of person is the prince? What words best describe him?

The Prince Who Went Alone

The Prince sat alone in the tower room, the only place in the royal palace where he could go by himself to think. He was reading a letter marked "Urgent—For His Royal Highness Only":

Success at last!—After searching for ten years, I have found the pirate's map that will lead you to your great-great-great-grandfather's stolen jewels. You can have the map if you will come alone to my fortress.

Grouchily yours,
Grumpus the Hermit

P.S. *Don't stay long. I hate company.*

The Prince gazed out the window. From high in the tower he could see the farms and villages of his country, and far in the distance was the world-famous National Library of Sights, Sounds, and Smells. The Prince knew the farmers and villagers needed new highways and bridges and schools, and the National Library could always use money to buy new recordings, films, and bottles of perfume. The pirate's map and the royal jewels were his for the asking—but first he would have to go to the hermit's fortress, and go alone.

"Grumpus the Hermit is the most loyal subject this country has ever had," said the prince to himself, "but for a hero, he certainly is a strange man. He absolutely refuses to see more than one person at a time." The Prince liked to talk to himself when he was alone. On most days he was surrounded by so many guards, royal relatives, diplomats, and reporters that he forgot what his own voice sounded like.

The Prince tiptoed down the long, winding tower staircase and tried to walk out the front gate of the palace. But the Sergeant of the Palace Detectives stopped him. "You can't leave these walls without your bodyguards," he said. "You might be kidnapped."

"I'm on a secret mission," said the Prince. "I order you to step aside."

"Absolutely not! It's against the law for a Palace Detective to let a Prince go out by himself."

The Prince went down into the basement. "Those guards of mine are just trying to do their job," he said, "but I'll fool them." He climbed out the window and swam across the moat. For the first time in his life, he was outside the palace, free and alone, without any guards. He was also soaking wet. "The pirate's map won't do me any good if I catch pneumonia," he said to himself. "I guess I'll have to buy myself some dry clothes."

As he was walking to the nearest clothing story, a group of people came strolling by on a walking tour. "Look!" exclaimed the tour director. "I don't believe it! It's his Royal Highness the Prince!"

"Quick! Let's all get his autograph!" shouted a tourist.

"I want to take his picture!" cried another, aiming his camera.

© Mark Twain Media, Inc., Publishers   53

"I want to be in the picture!" said somebody else. "Let's *all* get in the picture! Your Highness, wait for us!"

"I can't let the hermit see me with this crowd," muttered the Prince to himself. Even though he had never been outdoors by himself before, he had run many laps around the royal gymnasium, and he was a good sprinter. He dashed through the village with the tourists pounding behind him, snapping their cameras and waving their autograph books. The Prince saw a garden with a scarecrow dressed in a shabby coat and a floppy straw hat, and he had an idea. He grabbed the coat and hat, put them on, and stood perfectly still, pretending to be a scarecrow.

His trick worked. The tourists rushed past without recognizing him "This disguise is perfect!" said the Prince, dancing a little jig step. "Off I go to the hermit's fortress, all by myself!" Just then the scarecrow's owner came out of his house and stared at the Prince. "My scarecrow is bewitched!" he shouted. "It's dancing and walking by itself!"

The farmer's wife and his six tall sons came running. "Catch that scarecrow!" the wife shouted. "A dancing scarecrow will be worth a fortune. We can sell it to a circus!"

The Prince hated the idea of being sold to a circus. He ran faster than he had ever run in his life, with the farmer's six tall sons right on his heels, straight down the road to Friendly Fanny's Fine Fireworks Stand. The prince had another idea. He ducked into the fireworks stand and threw himself flat on the floor behind the counter. "They'll never look for me here," he thought to himself. "No scarecrow would dare to go into a building full of rockets and Roman candles. He'd be afraid of catching fire."

The farmer's sons hurried past without even pausing. Once again the Prince was alone—but not for long. Before he could get to his feet again, Friendly Fanny came running out of her office. "Poor man, you fainted dead away!" she cried. "You must be having a heart attack! Lie still and I'll call an ambulance."

"No, wait—you don't understand!" said the Prince. "All I want is to be alone!" But Fanny had already pushed the emergency number on her telephone.

The prince had never run so far or so fast in his life, and he was worn out from the effort, but he managed to jump to his feet and hurry out the door. In the distance he heard the ambulance sirens. Gasping for breath, he ran toward the National Library of Sights, Sounds, and Smells, looking for a new hiding place. Suddenly he heard the pounding of horses' hooves behind him. He whirled around and saw the Royal Mounted Guard thundering down the street.

"Emergency!" shouted the Captain. "Call the Army, the Navy, and the Air Force! The Prince is gone—*vanished*—KIDNAPPED! Question everybody! Start with that suspicious-looking man in the shabby coat and straw hat."

"I might as well give up," thought the Prince. "If the Mounted Guardsmen recognize me, they'll

Creative Writing PART SIX: Writing Your Story; Writing and Revising

lock me in the palace. And I'm too tired to run much farther. If only there were a way to make people stay away from me. . ."

Suddenly the answer came to him. With all the strength left in his body, he dashed into the National Library, raced through the wing marked SMELLS, and burst past a red-lettered sign that said I'D STAY AWAY IF I WERE YOU. "Stop!" shouted the chief librarian. *"Nobody* touches anything on those shelves!" The library guards closed in on the Prince, but he was too fast for them. He took a deep breath. Then he seized a bottle marked "Essence of Skunk," jerked the cork free, and poured the essence all over himself.

The library guards turned and ran, holding their noses. "Quick! Open all the windows!" shouted the head librarian. "Turn on all the fans!" In the confusion, the Prince escaped through a window.

For the rest of the day, nobody wanted to question the Prince, take him to a hospital, sell him to a circus, or ask for his autograph. Everyone stayed as far away from him as possible. Late that night he arrived at the front gate of the fortress. The Hermit stuck his head out of the window.

"Go away," he said. "You smell terrible."

"But at least I'm alone," said the Prince. He was holding his nose because he could hardly stand to smell himself.

"I'll fold the map into a paper airplane and sail it down to you," said the Hermit. "Just take it and go—*please!*"

When the Prince got back to the palace, he had to take three baths in tomato juice and vinegar, and even after that, nobody wanted to get close to him for a week. But he didn't mind. He had gotten used to the smell, and he enjoyed having some time alone to think.

Help yourself to plan a writing schedule by answering the following questions:

1. At what time or times of the day are you most alert? _____

2. Do you work best in a quiet place, or do you prefer a little background noise? _____

3. Do you like to listen to music while you work? _____

4. Do you usually feel satisfied with your first efforts, or do you prefer to revise? _____

5. Do you ever make an outline before you start to work? _____

6. During what hours are you free to write or study? Do you have any "waiting" times that could be used for writing? _____

7. Sometimes the most important part of writing is just thinking—planning a story in the mind. Do you like to think? Do you know of a pleasant place where you can sit or lie quietly and think about your schoolwork or other projects? _____

_____

_____

Creative Writing

PART SIX: WRITING YOUR STORY

26. Planning the Outline

There is a type of writer who is terrified of blank paper. He makes all sorts of excuses in order to avoid working, and when he is finally forced to write something—a letter, a paper for school, a poem, or a story—he sits helplessly at his desk, chewing his pen, listening to the clock tick, staring at those awful white sheets of paper. How will he ever be able to fill them with words? And—horror of horrors!—what if he has to sit there until dawn, waiting for words that never come?

A good way to overcome the fear of paper is to begin your project by making an outline. If you are writing a short story for the first time, you should probably make an outline whether you are afraid of blank paper or not. Otherwise, you may spend an hour writing a splendid episode, only to discover that it really has nothing to do with your plot. To begin your outline, write the title of your story at the top of a sheet of paper. (Or call it the "working title," because you may change your mind later on.) Then write the name of your protagonist and identify who or what the antagonists are. Next, make a brief outline of the five or six major scenes or developments in your plot. Because the outline is for your use only, you won't have to worry too much about its form.

An outline of "The Prince Who Went Alone" might look something like this:

I. The Prince reads a letter from the hermit and learns that he must visit the fortress alone in order to get the pirate's map.

II. The Prince escapes from the castle.
    A. Palace detectives try to stop him from leaving.
    B. He escapes by swimming the moat.

III. The Prince and the tourists
    A. On his way to a store to buy some dry clothes, he is surrounded by tourists who want to get his autograph and take his picture.
    B. He fools them by disguising himself as a scarecrow.

IV. The Prince as a scarecrow
    A. A farmer and his family think they have seen a dancing scarecrow and decide to sell him to a circus.
    B. The Prince hides in a fireworks stand.

V. Trouble at Friendly Fanny's Fine Fireworks
    A. Friendly Fanny thinks the Prince has had a heart attack and calls the ambulance.
    B. The Prince flees from the ambulance just as the Royal Mounted Guard closes in on him.

VI. Alone at last!
    A. The Prince runs into the National Library and douses himself with Essence of Skunk.
    B. He reaches the hermit's fortress and receives the map.
    C. Everyone leaves him alone for a week.

Creative Writing PART SIX: Writing Your Story; Planning the Outline

A good story should become more complicated and intense as it goes along. In "The Prince Who Went Alone," the protagonist encounters one problem after another until he is literally surrounded and almost ready to drop from exhaustion. But just when the situation looks hopeless, he has his big idea that finally allows him to be left in peace long enough to get his hands on that wonderful map.

People often ask, "How long should a story be?" There is no magic answer to this question; stories can range from a short joke to a three-volume novel. As a beginner, you should probably aim at something between 500 words (about two typewritten pages or three handwritten pages) and 1,500 words (about six typewritten pages or nine handwritten pages.) "The Prince Who Went Alone" is about 1,300 words long.

Creative Writing PART SIX: Writing Your Story; Planning the Outline

Date _____ Name _____

ASSIGNMENT: Making an Outline of Your Story

1. What do you think the title of your story will be?

_____

2. Write down the name of your protagonist.

_____

3. Who or what will the antagonists be?

_____

_____

4. What will the protagonist be doing when the story opens?

_____

_____

5. Write down three to six main stages in the conflict.

_____

_____

_____

_____

_____

_____

6. How will the protagonist finally solve his or her problem?

_____

_____

_____

_____

Creative Writing

PART SIX: WRITING YOUR STORY

27. Drawing the Characters

The more you know about your characters, the more vividly they will come to life. Many authors won't start writing a story or book until they have prepared a biography of the protagonist—and, in some cases, a biography of every other character as well. For example, if such a writer were planning a story entitled "Sarah Sees It Through," he might ask himself such questions as these: Where was Sarah born? What is her favorite food? her favorite song? her favorite book? What is she most afraid of, and what does she worry about? What color does she hate most? Where would be her dream vacation? The writer may not necessarily use all of this information in his story. What he is doing is getting to know and understand Sarah so that she will seem real to him—and eventually to his readers.

A biography of the Prince in "The Prince Who Went Alone" might contain the following bits and pieces of information: The Prince was born in the Royal Palace instead of in a hospital. When he was a student, his favorite subjects were art and history, but he did not much care for algebra. He hates the color purple (mainly because it is the traditional symbol of royalty and he gets tired of looking at it all day). He worries that he will turn bald as he grows older, and his greatest fear is of being trapped inside a burning building. On some days he enjoys his job as Prince—especially when he gets to listen to the music of a fine marching band—and he absolutely loves opening nights at the museum, but he feels uncomfortable when he has to make a speech. For exercise he runs and works out in the royal gymnasium, but he secretly dreams of hang gliding. His perfect vacation would be a safari to Africa, accompanied by a few trusty guides and a faithful elephant. None of this material actually turns up in the story, but such details help the author to understand his protagonist more clearly.

Must you write a biography of every character in the story? Probably not, unless your story includes only two characters: a protagonist and an antagonist. It would be a waste of time, for example, for the author of "The Prince Who Went Alone" to spend an hour writing a biography of Friendly Fanny, who appears only briefly in two short paragraphs. Should you write your biography in the form of an essay? You may if you wish, but some writers would be happy just to make a list of the character's likes, dislikes, hopes, wishes, fears, dreams, worries, and characteristics. Remember that the purpose of the biography is to help you write a good story, not to present a pleasing appearance on the page. Don't worry about neatness until you write the final draft of your story.

© Mark Twain Media, Inc., Publishers

Creative Writing — PART SIX: Writing Your Story; Drawing the Characters

Date _____ Name _____

ASSIGNMENT: A Biography of the Protagonist

1. Write the name of your protagonist: _____

2. Where was this character born? _____

3. What are the character's happiest and worst childhood memories?
_____

4. Does your character have a hobby or special interest? _____

5. List the character's favorite color, song, television program, book, food, and subject in school.
_____

6. What is he or she most afraid of?
_____

7. What is your protagonist's fondest daydream or wish?
_____
_____

8. What does he or she especially dislike?
_____

9. What are his or her best qualities?
_____
_____

10. What are the flaws in his or her character?
_____
_____

At last you have done the necessary preparation. You have set your schedule and made an outline of your story. You have a good understanding of your protagonist's character. The time has come to start writing.

GOOD LUCK!

Creative Writing

PART SEVEN: WHAT WRITERS DO

28. Writing a Book Review

If you enjoyed writing a short story, you might also like to explore some of the other fields in which writers work. Look around you, and you will discover that writers are everywhere: they teach classes, edit books, write articles for newspapers and magazines, prepare brochures and advertisements, do research and publish the results, send out newsletters—and in their spare time, they may amuse themselves by keeping diaries, writing letters, jotting down poetry, composing their own greeting cards, and serving as publicity chairmen for their favorite clubs and organizations.

The *book review* is an especially useful thing to learn about, and not just because teachers frequently assign book reports as homework projects. In the modern world, most people are busy, books are expensive, and the average reader is wary of spending time and money on a book unless he is reasonably certain of enjoying it. So almost every major magazine and newspaper publishes book reviews. Even a small-town weekly newspaper or school publication is likely to have a book review column.

If you want to be a good critic, you should review the kinds of books that you enjoy. If you hate sports, don't try to review a novel set in a baseball camp or a self-help book about perfecting the slam-dunk. If romances make you turn green, you are not the right person to review a best-seller entitled *Wild Passionate Promises*. For a critic, the usual advice applies: **"Write about what you know."** If you have worked on a rabbit farm, you might make the perfect reviewer for Richard Adams's *Watership Down* or Lynn Hall's *The Solitary*. Both of these novels deal with rabbits, and you would probably enjoy reading them, but you would also be in a position to know whether the information in the books is accurate.

Most book reviews are short, so unless your teacher has specifically asked for a ten-page paper, aim for about 200–500 words—and definitely no more than 800 words. Assume that your reader is an intelligent person *who has never read the book but might want to.* You can start by giving a little basic information (the title and author of the book, the general subject matter, reasons why the subject is important, perhaps an overall impression of the book) and a brief summary of the plot or the main ideas. (Remember: *Never give away the ending,* especially of a mystery!) Then you will have the tricky task of explaining why you liked or disliked the work.

If you thoroughly enjoyed the book, say so, but be sparing in your use of such words and phrases as *spectacular, awesome, spine-tingling, couldn't put it down, kept me on the edge of my seat,* and so on. A good critic should enjoy books but should also be thoughtful. Give specific reasons why you liked the book: the characters were appealing and believable, the plot was full of surprises, and the setting was so real that you could almost taste the ocean spray, feel the dampness of the fog, and hear the crash of waves against the shore.

If you disliked the book, you might as well be honest, but avoid such comments as "This book is the biggest disaster since the fall of the Roman Empire" or "This author is so empty-headed that his five-hundred-page book doesn't even make a good paperweight, let alone a doorstop." Instead, say that you couldn't respect the protagonist because she spent all of her time complaining instead of trying to solve her problems, that the villain was too evil to be believed, and that the plot seemed to fizzle out in the last two chapters. And just to prove that you are a fair-minded person, try to think of at least one positive comment. Maybe you thought the book was worth reading in spite of serious flaws. If so, explain as clearly as possible and leave your reader to make his or her own decision about whether to read the book.

What if your assigned book is a classic, a masterpiece, one of the glories of literature—and you hated it from start to finish? Fear not; no rule says you have to love every classic that was ever written. If you loathed *The Last of the Mohicans,* you can't very well say that it's stupid and worthless; after all, people have been enjoying it for over a hundred and fifty years. But you can say that the narrow escapes were hard to believe, that you found the violence distasteful, that the heroines were too perfect to be true, that the story would have been more exciting if the author had eliminated some unnecessary description and dialogue, or that the ending was an unpleasant surprise. There are plenty of sensible reasons not to like *The Last of the Mohicans*.

ASSIGNMENT: Writing a Book Review

Go to a library or bookstore and choose a book that you think you would enjoy. Read it and write a brief review, explaining why this book should or should not be purchased for the school library.

Creative Writing

PART SEVEN: WHAT WRITERS DO

29. Writing a Short Newspaper Article

People often wonder how to "break in" to professional writing. The easiest way to get started is by writing short articles for newspapers and newsletters. You probably won't get paid a penny for your efforts, but you will have the satisfaction of seeing your words in print and hearing your friends say, "Hey, I saw your story in the paper." You will also gain practice, experience, and confidence from writing for a news publication.

What is a good subject for a short article? Some newspapers print regular reports from clubs and organizations, especially if a group is sponsoring an awards banquet, a contest, or a speech by a prominent individual. Newspapers also publish stories about leading citizens and about ordinary people who do unusual things. (I once wrote a newspaper article about a drama teacher who built a flying, fire-breathing dragon as part of the scenery for a college play.) Newspapers can use book reviews (as we learned in the last chapter), and they also print movie reviews, record reviews, and reviews of plays and shows. The so-called "How-to-do-it" article is always popular, and it can deal with almost any interest you might have.

Where can you publish a short article? Well, you may not be ready for the *New York Times* or the *Wall Street Journal* yet, but check your local newspaper to see whether it has a weekly feature called "Youth's Perspective" or "Focus on Teens." Check your favorite magazines, too, and see whether one of them has a "From the Readers" page. Or maybe you belong to a church or an organization that prints its own newsletter or bulletin. Does your school have a student newspaper? If not, perhaps your teachers will help you start one.

Two brief warnings: First, whatever you write for a newspaper should be *true.* If you become careless with facts, you will get a bad reputation, and no one will believe what you write. So check your facts, and then check them again. Second, articles about friends, neighbors, and ordinary people should be not only true but also kind. If you are writing a review of a terrible movie, go ahead and express your displeasure; Hollywood filmmakers are supposed to know what they are doing. But in a review of the seventh-grade ballet class's production of the *Nutcracker,* you don't necessarily have to mention that the orchestra was out of tune, that the Christmas tree toppled over, and that the Sugar Plum Fairy fell off the stage during her big dance. Just say that the dancers put forth a great deal of effort, that the costumes were beautiful, and that the *Nutcracker* is one of the most popular ballets ever composed.

© Mark Twain Media, Inc., Publishers

Creative Writing   PART SEVEN: What Writers Do; Writing a Short Newspaper Article

Date _____ Name _____

ASSIGNMENT: Ideas for Newspaper Articles

1. Do you belong to an organization that has an annual awards dinner or other special occasion?
_____

2. Do you know anyone who has an unusual hobby or collection, who has recently traveled to an out-of-the-way place, or who has built or made something special?
_____

3. Do you have a friend who has won a contest such as a spelling bee or received some kind of award or honor? What do you suppose your friend had to do in order to win?
_____
_____
_____

4. Do you like to go to plays, concerts, or recitals? Would you enjoy the life of a drama or music critic?
_____

5. Have you seen an unusually good or bad movie lately? What was it?
_____

6. What sports do you attend regularly? If you were going to write a sports article for a newspaper, which sport would you choose?
_____
_____
_____

7. Can you bake a cake, develop your own photographs, play the guitar? Do you have a skill that people might like to learn? What advice could you give to somebody who wants to succeed at your special skill?
_____
_____
_____
_____

Study a few short newspaper articles and then write an article of your own based on one of the above ideas. Who knows; maybe your class can publish a newspaper of its own!

Creative Writing

PART SEVEN: WHAT WRITERS DO

30. The Dreaded Research Paper!

Sooner or later it will happen to *you:* just as you are starting to look forward to summer vacation, a teacher with an ominous gleam in his eye will demand that you write a research paper before school is out. Your first reaction will be panic. What on Earth is a research paper? What does this teacher *want*, anyway? And how can you possibly get it finished before June and still have time to learn your clarinet solo for the annual Spring Fling?

A research paper is one of the most challenging assignments that a student can face, because it requires the student to (1) learn a considerable amount of information by reading, and (2) write down what he or she has learned in a completely new form. A research paper often seems to be a nuisance because the writer has to follow a specific format and deal with such headaches as footnotes, citations, bibliographies, lists of "Works Cited," proper margins, and long and short quotations. The first time you write a research paper, you may feel that this assignment is tedious busywork at best and at worst an instrument of torture that ought to be blacklisted by Amnesty International.

Nevertheless, the ability to write a good research paper is an important and even necessary skill. If you go to college, you will find that many professors require a term paper as part of the normal work of the course, and if you become a teacher, a doctor, a lawyer, or a scientist, you will almost certainly have to do research as a part of your job. Furthermore, if the research paper is the most difficult of assignments, it is also the most rewarding, because it will expose you to a variety of facts and opinions and teach you to think for yourself. After you have written several good research papers, you will discover that you have a mind of your own and you know how to use it.

If you are a student in a junior high or middle school, it may be a year or two before you are assigned a research paper. When that assignment finally comes, the most important thing to remember is that you will write a better paper if you **choose a subject that is interesting to you.** If you hate reptiles, don't write a paper about snakes just because you have heard that your teacher has a snake sanctuary in his backyard. Even if your teacher loves snakes better than he loves his own children, he surely doesn't want to spend all of his waking hours reading about snakes, and he will be impressed if you can teach him something that he doesn't already know. Besides, how can your snake paper possibly be any good if you can't think about the project without feeling sick?

Likewise, don't feel that you have to write about the Louisiana Purchase or the life of George Washington just because such subjects seem "important." Why not write a paper about Jesse James if you are fascinated with outlaws and bandits? Or about the old Mississippi steamboats if you love to travel? Or about wolf packs if you like animals and nature?

Another thing to remember is that you should *limit* your topic. A research paper is supposed to be a detailed study, not a sketch, and you can't write a detailed study of "The Civil War" or "The Life and Works of Mark Twain" in five or six pages. But you could write a paper about the battle of Gettysburg or about Mark Twain's boyhood in Missouri or about how Harriet Beecher Stowe's book *Uncle Tom's Cabin* aroused anger against slavery.

Your teacher will give you instructions on the correct use of citations, the bibliography, quotations, and so on. You should follow these instructions carefully and make your paper look as attractive as possible. If your paper is typed or printed with an old ribbon, and if you leave no margins and use paper flimsy enough to see through, you will have no right to complain if you receive a poor grade. On the other hand, a handsome manuscript, typescript, or print-out reflects pride in yourself and your work. It says, "I cared enough about this assignment to give my best effort."

Creative Writing   PART SEVEN: What Writers Do; The Dreaded Research Paper

Date _____ Name _____

ASSIGNMENT: Thinking About Projects for Research

1. What is your favorite subject in school?
_____
_____

2. Suppose that you were asked to write a research paper for this class. What are some topics that you might find interesting to explore?
_____
_____
_____
_____
_____
_____
_____

3. Do any of these topics need to be limited or narrowed down? Can you think of ways to limit them?
_____
_____
_____
_____
_____
_____

4. Where could you find information about one of your topics?
_____
_____
_____
_____
_____
_____
_____
_____

Creative Writing

PART SEVEN: WHAT WRITERS DO

31. Writing About Your Opinions

All of us have opinions about everything under the sun. Most of us think we know the best way to tell a joke; we also have opinions about how the President of the United States should lead the country. Some of us even believe that we have discovered the secret to achieving world peace.

Some writers are paid for their opinions. An editor of a newspaper typically includes an *editorial* in every issue. Other writers may have their opinions published in newspapers around the country; we call these people "columnists," or we say that they "write commentary." You may be familiar with some of their names: George Will, Ellen Goodman, Anna Quindlen, William Raspberry, Anthony Lewis. A few columnists, like Erma Bombeck and Mike Royko, offer their opinions with a humorous twist.

If you think you would like to be a columnist, you might try testing your wings by writing a letter to an editor. Opportunities are plentiful: almost every magazine or newspaper has a "letters" column. Some newspapers and magazines also publish commentaries by young readers. Check your favorite magazine or newspaper to find out what the requirements are.

Choose a subject that is important to you—but if you are truly angry about an issue, it would be a good idea to wait a day or two and get your temper under control before you fire off a letter to the newspaper. And no matter how strong your feelings may be, your commentary will be more persuasive if you adopt a reasonable, responsible tone. Remember that even a newborn infant can complain at the top of its lungs, but only a mature man or woman can propose a sensible solution to a problem. Remember too that the majority of people, whatever their failings may be, are men and women of good will who are trying to do the right thing in the best way they know how. So don't be too quick to condemn a person just because his opinion is different from yours.

For example, suppose that the mayor and council of your city have just issued a new policy on lawn clippings and yard waste. You are afraid that the new policy may force you to give up your after-school lawn-mowing business, and you need the money to buy materials for school. So you sit down to write a letter of protest: *"As usual, the mayor and the city council acted like a pack of idiots when they passed the stupid and dangerous new regulations on lawn clippings. With "city fathers" like these, our town would be better off as an orphan. The mayor and his pals should retire from politics and get jobs as circus clowns—but no; on second thought, they might find clowning too much of a strain on their so-called minds. Besides, a good clown has to have a little kindness and decency in his heart."*

Writing this letter might make you feel better, but when you have finished it, you should tear it up and throw it in the wastebasket. You can't win people to your side by insulting them. As a citizen, however, you have a perfect right to express your opinion on lawn clippings or anything else. You might begin your letter like this: *"The members of the city council have presented several good reasons for their new policy on yard waste. Nevertheless, I believe that this policy will do more harm than good. In the first place . . . ."* Or, if you wish to be more brief: *"I am opposed to the new policy on yard waste for the following reasons . . . ."* The use of humor or fantasy will allow you to make your point without hurting anyone's feelings: *"Yesterday while I was mowing the lawn, my father's tractor sputtered, coughed, shuddered to a halt, and gave up. It must have heard about the city's new policy on grass clippings. I can understand how it feels because . . ."* Notice that your argument will be stronger if you concentrate on the grass-clipping issue, not on the personalities and intellects of the mayor and the council.

A good piece of commentary should reveal the mind and character of the author, but it should not sound conceited or selfish. So avoid using the words *I*, *me*, *my*, and *mine* in every sentence. If you state your beliefs clearly, your reader will get a sense of who you are. Also, remember that you can have opinions about anything, not just the "important" and serious problems of the world. One of Ellen Goodman's best (and funniest) columns was about a pair of smoke detectors that refused to work correctly.

So think about the problems, major and minor, that you encounter in your daily life: a lost kitten, a broken window, bad sportsmanship at a basketball game, unfair and hurtful gossip in the hallways of your school, and so on. Think too about the people in your life who deserve praise: parents, coaches, Scout leaders, hard workers, and good citizens of all sorts. You will never run out of material for commentary.

Date _____ Name _____

ASSIGNMENT: Taking Stock of Your Opinions

1. What problems do you face on a typical day?
_____
_____

2. Have you ever seen or experienced something that seemed unfair to you? What?
_____
_____

3. What would you do to improve your school, your neighborhood, or your town?
_____
_____

4. Does it irritate you when things break down or refuse to work properly?
_____

5. Do you know anyone who deserves a few words of appreciation? Who?
_____

6. Are there any news stories that interest you? List a few.
_____
_____

Pretend you are a columnist for a major newspaper and write an imaginary column about something that is important to you.

Creative Writing

PART SEVEN: WHAT WRITERS DO

32. Doing an Interview

Everyone is fascinated by interesting people. For many writers, an important part of the job is to conduct conversations, or *interviews,* with people who have done important or unusual things. There are a number of reasons why you might want to interview someone: you might be doing research for a work of fiction or a term paper, or you might be seeking information for a newspaper article. You might even want to write an entire paper or article about a friend who has lived in Senegal or who won the state kite-flying championship. In some fields, such as psychology, a good scholar can learn as much from people as from books.

When you prepare for an interview, you must keep one thing foremost in your mind: *The person whom you interview is doing you a favor,* not the other way around, so always be considerate. Never call somebody at eight o'clock on a Friday morning and say, "My paper is due at nine this morning; I have to come over right now and do an interview with you." If your subject agrees to talk with you at all, you will find him in an angry mood when you arrive at his home or office. Instead, contact him several days before your project is due. Don't tell him that you "have to" do an interview; most people resent being summoned or ordered around. Explain what kind of project you are doing and ask whether he would be willing to talk with you. If he agrees, set the interview for a time and place that is convenient for both of you. Unless the interview is with your own grandmother or best friend, it is probably a bad idea to invite yourself to your subject's house.

If your subject is an alligator farmer and you know nothing about alligators, it might be a good idea to do a little reading about them before you go to the interview. Then think of five or six questions that you would like to ask the farmer and jot them down. This simple trick will save you the problem of awkward silences as you try desperately to think of a good question. When you go to the interview, be on time and be friendly and polite. Remember—the farmer is doing you a favor by agreeing to help you with your project.

How should you take notes on an interview? Some writers might want to use a tape recorder, but even in this age of camcorders and tape decks, many people are still afraid to have their voices recorded. You might think that an alligator farmer would be fearless, but people's fears are often illogical. Besides, you can save time by taking notes during the interview. A legal pad would be a good tool.

© Mark Twain Media, Inc., Publishers

Creative Writing PART SEVEN: What Writers Do; Doing an Interview

Taking notes while carrying on a conversation is a difficult skill that requires practice. A good professional reporter can actually "take notes" in his head and then write them down on paper immediately after the interview is over. You should probably not try this on your first interview, but don't take so many notes that your conversation never has a chance to get interesting.

Don't overstay your welcome, no matter how much you enjoy the alligator farm. Before you leave, thank the farmer politely, and if it seems appropriate, send him a thank-you note. Then write your story, and remember to be fair and accurate. Few things are more upsetting than to read lies about oneself in the newspaper. You might be able to write a more exciting story by stretching the truth—by claiming that some of the alligators have escaped into the sewer system and the city lake, for example— but if you get a reputation for dishonesty, you will soon find that no one is willing to grant you an interview or give you any information.

A particularly awful form of dishonesty is *quoting out of context*. It works like this: an exterminator says to a reporter, "When I see a house that's crawling and swarming with termites and roaches, I just can't wait to kill every living creature in sight." The next day the exterminator's picture appears in the newspaper alongside a big black headline: *"I just can't wait to kill every living creature in sight!"* Thus an honest, hardworking exterminator has been transformed into a maniac.

For interviewing and doing other kinds of research, the best rule is the Golden Rule: *Always treat others as you would have them treat you.*

Date _____ Name _____

ASSIGNMENT: Interviewing

Interview a friend, relative, or classmate who has done something you find interesting. Write a short essay based on the interview.

Write an imaginary interview with a famous historical or fictional character.

1. What famous person would you most like to interview? What questions would you ask him or her?

_____
_____
_____
_____
_____
_____

Creative Writing

PART SEVEN: WHAT WRITERS DO

33. Keeping a Diary

A *diary* or *journal* is an account of one's day-to-day experiences. Keeping a diary is good practice for a beginning writer, partly because it will get him used to the discipline of doing a little writing every day. You can buy a cloth-bound diary at a greeting card store, or you can use an ordinary notebook. A modern diarist might prefer to keep a computer disk with the label "My Diary" or "Daily Journal."

There are many kinds of diaries. The simplest type is just a brief record of the events of each day; such a diary might not even be written in complete sentences. The entire entry for March 3 might go like this: "Bought a new sweater and some gloves at Miller's Department Store. It rained all morning, everything clear by afternoon. Aunt Elizabeth called, said she will come for a week's visit on April 10." Not very interesting reading, but useful to have on hand in case you should forget exactly when Aunt Elizabeth plans to arrive or where you should return that sweater if it starts to unravel. If you want to keep this sort of record, buy a five-year diary at a card or stationery store. If you prefer to go into more detail, a one-year diary would be a better choice.

When a writer keeps a diary (which she usually calls a *journal*), she is less interested in events than in impressions. She sees a gorgeous sunset, and she knows that someday she will need to describe the setting sun in one of her stories. She grabs her journal notebook and writes a vivid description of the sunset before it can fade away. If an idea for a story pops into her head, she jots that down too; otherwise, she may awaken the next morning to discover that the wonderful idea has popped right out of her head—gone forever, without a trace left behind.

A third type of diary is a record of thoughts and ideas. Columnists, preachers, lecturers, and thinkers in general like to keep such journals in order to collect material for sermons, speeches, articles, and books.

Diaries are important historical records. By reading diaries that have been saved over the decades and centuries, we can understand what it was like to live in a distant time or place. Some people have become famous because of their diaries. During the seventeenth century, an English gentleman named Samuel Pepys (pronounced "peeps") kept a lively record of his life in London; his diary is still fun to read. Mary Chesnut wrote a diary about her life as a southern woman during the Civil War. One of the most famous modern diaries was written by Anne Frank, a young Jewish girl who lived with her family in hiding from the Nazis during World War II. Anne died in a concentration camp, but her diary was saved and published, and it continues to be read by people around the world.

A person like Anne Frank may look upon her diary as a kind of friend and companion. But if you are confiding your deepest thoughts to your diary, you must be careful to keep it in a safe place at all times. What if somebody were to steal your diary, make photocopies of the most private entries, and circulate them around the school? Such things have been known to happen (Samuel Pepys kept his diary in code, just in case). If you don't have a safe place to hide a diary, perhaps you should stick to a record of events and impressions and leave your innermost thoughts locked safely inside your heart.

Creative Writing   PART SEVEN: What Writers Do; Keeping a Diary

Date _____ Name _____

ASSIGNMENT: Your Diary

Try keeping a diary or journal for one week. You can decide whether to record events, impressions, ideas, or some of each, and you may use extra paper if you like.

First Day _____
_____
_____

Second Day _____
_____
_____

Third Day _____
_____
_____

Fourth Day _____
_____
_____

Fifth Day _____
_____
_____

Sixth Day _____
_____
_____

Seventh Day _____
_____
_____

© Mark Twain Media, Inc., Publishers

Creative Writing

PART SEVEN: WHAT WRITERS DO

34. Writing Letters

Back in the eighteenth century, telephones did not exist, and travel was difficult and dangerous. Even if automobiles could have been imported on a time machine, there would have been no fine highways where one could drive. About the only way to keep in touch with absent friends or relatives was to write letters. And just as Samuel Pepys became famous for his diary, so a number of eighteenth-century writers became famous for their long and beautifully written letters to friends and relatives. In England, for example, a man called Lord Chesterfield wrote an entire book of letters to his son, and in America, Thomas Jefferson and John Adams shared their ideas in a long series of letters that are now famous.

If Adams and Jefferson had lived in the 1980s, however, they might never have written any letters at all. If Adams had had something to say to Jefferson, he would have picked up the telephone, or Jefferson would have hopped in his car and driven to Adams's house. In 1980, the old-fashioned letter seemed to be as obsolete as the stagecoach. And why not? Why should Jefferson and Adams fuss around with paper and stamps if they could hear each other's voices over the telephone or see each other in person?

A telephone call is easier than a letter; it travels faster, and it puts people in closer contact. But telephone calls can't be saved and read again; they can't be shared with friends a week later; they can't be collected in museums for historians to study; and they certainly can't be published for the world to read. And although one might like to have a "pen pal" in Australia, an Australian "telephone pal" would be impossibly expensive. Besides, telephone calls always seem to come when one is watching a favorite television program or taking a bath.

Is the letter going the way of the dinosaur? Don't count on it! Technology, which once threatened to destroy the art of letter writing, may soon make the letter even more popular than it was during the eighteenth century. The facsimile or "fax" machine can send a letter across the Atlantic Ocean at the speed of a telephone call instead of in five or ten days. Even more exciting is electronic mail, or "E-mail," which allows people around the world to exchange letters through their personal computers. You could send an electronic message to your Australian pen pal and get an answer back the same day—and print a copy to read to your geography class. Jefferson and Adams would have loved E-mail.

Letters, like diaries, can be dangerous. If you have a message that must be kept private, you can't send it on a fax machine. Your letter will simply roll off the machine and onto a table (or maybe onto the floor), where it might sit for hours. You really have no idea who might pick it up and read it. Electronic mail also has its drawbacks. Computers are not perfect; a message can sometimes appear on the wrong screen. If you need privacy, a sealed envelope is still your best choice—and even then, you should think carefully about what you write. Believe it or not, your letter might fall into the hands of your grandchildren some day. It could even wind up in a museum!

© Mark Twain Media, Inc., Publishers

Creative Writing — PART SEVEN: What Writers Do; Writing Letters

Date _____ Name _____

ASSIGNMENT: Thinking About Letters

1. Do you know anyone who would enjoy receiving a letter from you? Who?
_____

2. Have you ever received a letter so special that you saved it?
_____

3. Have you ever received a letter that made you laugh? What was it about?
_____
_____
_____

4. What was the best news you ever received in a letter?
_____
_____
_____

5. What sorts of information might be dangerous to write in a letter?
_____
_____
_____

6. Does your school or library own a fax machine? Have you ever seen it at work?
_____

7. Does your school have a computer that can send electronic letters? Is there such a computer in your home?
_____

On your own paper, write an imaginary letter to a famous historical or fictional person, giving him advice or warning him to be careful. (Examples: Explain to Rip Van Winkle why he should stay at home instead of taking a walk in the Catskill Mountains, or explain to General Custer why he should give up his military career and open a barbecue restaurant.)

© Mark Twain Media, Inc., Publishers

Creative Writing

PART SEVEN: WHAT WRITERS DO

35. Getting Published

If you enjoyed some of your writing assignments, you have probably begun wondering about the chances of getting published in a book or magazine. Could such a thing happen to you? Dare you dream of it? And how do you get an editor's attention?

If you think you are ready to submit your work for publication, there are a number of possible destinations for your manuscripts. We have already considered the short newspaper article and the letter to the editor. Or maybe your school has its own literary magazine. In addition, some magazines publish stories, essays, and poems by young authors. *Highlights for Children*, for example, has a section called "Our Own Pages" that features poems and short stories from the readers, and *Seventeen* magazine has a feature called "Voice." *Merlyn's Pen*, *Stone Soup*, and *New Moon* are magazines that publish the work of young writers. For other ideas, check the magazine rack at a good newsstand or library, or consult your librarian.

When you write for publication, it is important to submit an attractive manuscript, because sloppy scripts are often returned unread to the author. Editors receive a great many submissions, and they may not feel that they have time to spend on a writer who can't be bothered to proofread his work and prepare a neat copy. Also, be sure to observe any guidelines. It is a waste of time and postage, for example, to send a ten-page story to a magazine that has a limit of five hundred words. And don't send a short story to a magazine that publishes only poetry, or an article about drag racing to a magazine that publishes only religious material. When you mail a manuscript, always include a self-addressed stamped envelope (called a SASE) so that the editor may return your material to you.

Now comes the hard part: Once you have put your manuscript in the mail, be prepared to wait patiently for several weeks or even several months. For an editor, choosing material for publication can be a slow process. It is a waste of your time and energy to fret, worry, and wonder about the fate of your story. So as soon as you put your manuscript in the mailbox, forget about it and start work on your next project. This is what professional writers do.

Be prepared to accept rejection. Few writers succeed without first collecting a drawer full of so-called rejection slips, and even a best-selling professional will get a rejection now and then. Rejection notices come in many shapes and sizes, but usually they arrive in the mail as form letters or little postcard-sized notes (hence the name "rejection slip"). Usually these notes are worded politely: *"We are sorry, but your manuscript does not meet our needs at the present time. We wish you every success in placing it elsewhere."*

"But why doesn't the editor at least explain why she doesn't like my story or my article?" you may ask. Alas, the editor is so busy working on her magazine that she doesn't have time to be a writing teacher too. Besides, editors often have to reject material that they like perfectly well, just because they don't have enough space to publish everything. Most of the time, a rejection slip means exactly what it says: "This does not meet our needs." The editor has nothing against you personally.

Rejection is sometimes painful, but don't let it stop you. Keep writing and sending your material through the mail, and sooner or later—with talent, hard work, and a little luck—you will be a published writer!

© Mark Twain Media, Inc., Publishers

Creative Writing — PART SEVEN: What Writers Do; Getting Published

Date _____ Name _____

ASSIGNMENT: Writing for Publication

1. Go to a library or newsstand where there is a collection of magazines for young readers, and look at these publications carefully. Study any magazines that may be lying around your school, home, or church. Which of these magazines have pages or sections devoted to young authors?

_____
_____
_____
_____

2. Do any of them have guidelines as to word length, subject matter, or manuscript form? If so, what are some of the guidelines?

_____
_____
_____
_____
_____
_____
_____

3. Which magazine would you be most likely to write for? How would you address a letter to this magazine?

_____
_____
_____
_____
_____
_____
_____

Do you have any material that you would like to submit for publication? If so, prepare a neat-looking copy and mail it to the editor.

GOOD LUCK, AND KEEP WRITING!

Creative Writing

PART SEVEN: WHAT WRITERS DO

36. Postscript—The Writers' Club

Writing is a lonely business. Instead of working in a busy office as most people do, a writer spends his hours in an empty room, staring at a computer screen or a piece of paper. It's only natural that sometimes he feels the urge to shut off his computer or put down his pen, get out of the house or library, and talk to other writers. Maybe they can give him help in revising a story that has somehow fallen flat. Besides, his fellow writers have valuable information that he needs—the news about a brand new publishing company, for example, or an editor who has a new position and needs manuscripts. For these reasons, writers often form clubs, which they may call *guilds* or *support groups.*

The usual business of such a group is for the members to share their work and offer encouragement or suggestions for revision. Many writers find these groups to be extremely helpful, and sometimes a new writer is able to launch a career because of the support of a writers' group. But such a club has to be managed carefully, or it can turn into a major disappointment. If you and some of your friends would like to form a writers' club, here are some pointers to keep in mind:

Club members can share their material in two ways: either by sending out copies before the meeting or by having the authors read aloud during the meeting. The first method gives members a chance to think about the material and have comments ready; the second method gives authors a chance to practice an important skill. (Successful writers, after all, are often called upon to give "readings.") Why not enjoy all the advantages and use both methods at once?

Meetings should definitely *start on time whether everyone is present or not.* If you spend too much time waiting around, your writers' group might turn into a social club, and no work will ever get done. Make sure that everyone gets a chance to speak and that no one talks for too long. At some point, you may find it necessary to set time limits. It will be the death of your group if one member talks endlessly or tries to run everything.

Criticism should be kind. If you are a member of a writers' group, you should try to find at least one thing to like about every manuscript. Be as specific and as helpful as you can. Instead of saying, "I just loved this story," say "The descriptions were beautiful" or "Page four is really funny" or "your villain is so creepy, I just wanted to smack him!" When you make suggestions for improvement, be gentle. Don't say, "I just couldn't understand the part about the green canoe; the whole thing was stupid, and I think you should throw that page away." Instead, try something like this: "If you want to revise this story, maybe you should explain a little more about the green canoe. I didn't quite understand how that canoe got to be in the pond."

When your own work is under discussion, listen politely, take notes if you wish, but don't try to defend yourself. This may seem hard and even unfair, but you'll find that the meetings will be much more pleasant if people avoid getting into debating contests or arguments. After the meeting, think carefully about any suggestions for improvement, but remember: *You don't have to follow a single one of them.* What you finally decide to do with your work—revise it completely, make a few changes, leave it as it is, or throw it away—is entirely up to you.

Meetings should end on time. Nobody loves a meeting that seems to be rambling on with no end in sight. If everyone has agreed to stop at four o' clock and four o'clock has arrived, the president or leader should stand up and say something like this: "Our time is up, and if you need to leave, you can go now. But anybody who wants to can stay and talk some more." In this way, people who are tired or busy will have a chance to leave, and club members will know that they can come to a meeting without being trapped for hours.

In addition to forming clubs, writers also like to attend *writers' conferences* or *writers' workshops.* A conference gives a writer the chance to travel to a distant city or state, meet editors and other writers, attend speeches and discussions about writing, and have his own work reviewed by a professional. If a writer wants to do a great deal of work in a short time, he may reserve a room or cottage at a *writers' retreat.* This is a quiet place, far away from telephones and other distractions, where a writer can work all day without being interrupted except by the person who brings him a little food. When his work is over for the day, he can spend the evening making friends with the other guests at the retreat. As you can see, a writer doesn't have to be lonely *all* of the time!

GROUP PROJECT: A Writers' Club

Organize the class into small groups and let each group hold a meeting as a "writer's club." Each club can choose a leader and come up with a name. It might be best to have a specific person assigned to give a review of each submission, with comments from the members to follow.